THE THREE MUSICIANS

Music therapy session in a psychiatric hospital. The patient playing the
violin made the instrument himself in the hospital workshop

MUSIC THERAPY

Juliette Alvin

MUSIC THERAPY

JOHN BAKER

5 ROYAL OPERA ARCADE,
PALL MALL, LONDON
SW 1.

Printed in Great Britain by
W. & J. Mackay & Co Ltd, Chatham, Kent

TO
W.A.R.

Acknowledgements

I wish to express my thanks to a number of people and organisations who kindly provided me with material with which to illustrate this book. Among them are the National Association for Mental Health, the Physicians Superintendents of several psychiatric hospitals, the *Nursing Times*, the Wingfield Music Club, Mrs Sydney Mitchell, Mrs E. A. Gluck, Mr Geoffrey Smales and Professor Jacques Millot.

I am indebted to Miss Muriel Davidson for reading the manuscript and making many very valuable comments.

I should like to add that the American National Association for Music Therapy and my own British Society for Music Therapy have been for many years a source of knowledge and inspiration without which this book could not have been written.

J.A.

Contents

PART TWO

THE MODERN APPLICATION OF MUSIC IN MEDICAL TREATMENT

Illustrations

PART ONE

HISTORICAL BACKGROUND

INTRODUCTION

THIS book is an attempt to present and integrate a new subject allied to a number of disciplines. The very name of Music Therapy calls to the mind diverse images and ideas. The following definition may help to describe a vast field little explored and not yet integrated.

Music Therapy is the controlled use of music in the treatment, rehabilitation, education and training of adults and children suffering from physical, mental and emotional disorder. Since it is a function of music in which music is not an end in itself, its therapeutic value is not necessarily related to the kind of music used, nor to the standard of musical achievement. Its effect is primarily due to the influence of sound on man, of which music was born, and whose curative, harmful or negative value will become apparent as our story unfolds throughout history. We will also observe that at all times music has created infinite kinds of relationships. Those form the corner-stone of music therapy.

The word 'music' applies to such a multiplicity of experiences that we should first try to unravel the many threads that weave its patterns and go far back to its origin. Then we may be able to understand at a basic human level why and how we can use music as a therapeutic agent. Music to the modern man is a finished complex product made of many elements combined together and in a state of everchanging temporal relationship. Each of these musical elements is an attribute of the substance of sound, a substance that has always been part of the conscious world of man and which he has interpreted or used according to his kind or state of civilisation.

We propose to include in this rapid historical survey only data that may be today related to the development of our Western music. Our music has scarcely been influenced by that of the East, which is based on a completely different musical system and philosophy.

I

The Origin of Music

1. THE COSMIC ORIGIN OF SOUND

MAN has sometimes believed that sound was a cosmic elemental force present at the beginning of the world and taking a verbal form. St John begins the first chapter of his Gospel with these words: 'In the beginning was the Word and the Word was with God and the Word was God' (John i. 1.).

We find a number of legends on the creation of the Universe in which sound played a major part. The Egyptians believed that the god 'Thot' had created the world not by thought or action but by his voice alone. From his mouth and the sounds it produced four other gods had been born, who were endowed with similar power and who had then peopled and organised the world.[1]

Marius Schneider states that in the philosophic conceptions deriving from Persian and Hindu cosmogonies the Universe had been created from an acoustical substance. He says: 'The world is supposed to have been created by an initial sound which when it emerged from the primordial abyss became light, and little by little part of this light became matter. But this materialisation was never absolutely complete because each material thing or object continued to retain more or less some of the sonorous substance out of which it was created.'[2]

[1] J. Combarieu, *La Musique et la Magie*, A. Picard & fils, Paris (1909), p. 126.
[2] Marius Schneider, 'Les Fondements intellectuels et psychologiques du Chant Magique', *Colloques de Wegimont*, Pub. Elsevier, Brussels (1956), p. 61. Author's translation.

The early Babylonians and ancient Greeks related sound to the cosmos through a mathematical conception of sound vibrations connected with numbers and astrology. 'Pythagorean philosophers', says Peter Crossley-Holland, 'conceived the musical scales as a structural element in the cosmos.'[1]

They also believed that although sound existed as a natural element in the universe it might not be perceptible to human ears. They called 'harmony of the spheres' the inaudible sounds produced by the movement of celestial bodies which expressed the mathematical harmony of the macrocosm.

The same idea that celestial sounds might be inaudible to human ears existed also in religious beliefs, but it was entirely mystical and had no scientific foundation. Man has sometimes believed that music from the divine Heaven could be heard and captured, but only by divinely inspired men. The Christian Byzantine composer was taught that 'the prototype of the religious melodies was the song of praise of the angels, inaudible to human ears but transmitted and made audible by the inspired hymnographers'.[2]

At all times, inspirations, revelations and hallucinations have been difficult to distinguish from one another. They are extrasensory phenomena, and often connected with mental disorder. Sound can be a source of delusion, through which man, primitive or civilised, sane or insane, has tried to communicate with an invisible psychic world.

From the Renaissance to our days the beliefs in the relation between sound and cosmos have remained in the field of intellectual or metaphysical speculation. Nevertheless their mathematical relationship can have emotional connotation for some writers who speak of 'the celestial logic of Bach'.[3]

[1] Peter Crossley-Holland, 'Non-Western Music—Greece', *Pelican History of Music*, p. 100.
[2] Egon Wellesz, *New Oxford History of Music*, Vol. 2, p. 43.
[3] Lord Brain, *The Nature of Experience*, O.U.P., p. 56.

We should not forget that some *avant-garde* composers of today base their musical compositions on mathematical combinations, calculated on electronic apparatus. Thus we enter a new musical world in which one day, perhaps, man may find a therapeutic element, if mathematical objective truth can be therapeutic. Already electronic music has opened a new field of interest to therapists, because it enables man to communicate with a world outside human emotions and symbols.

2. SOUND AND MAGIC

Primitive man explained natural phenomena in terms of magic and thought that sound was of supernatural origin. 'Sound', says Alfred Einstein, 'must have been to the primitive man something incomprehensible and therefore mysterious and magical.'[1] We may believe that to him sound expressed the mood, threats or orders from the spirits surrounding him. It was a means of communication with and from the invisible but ever-present world and it carried with it an unmistakable identity. This phenomenon has been observed in many parts of the world. According to Margaret Mead, certain primitive tribes in New Guinea believe that the voice of the spirits can be heard through the flutes, the drum and the bull roarer.[2]

This process is of particular interest in music therapy, especially when it leads to the identification of a human being with a specific sound. Marius Schneider tells us that especially in totemic civilisations there was a widespread belief that each of the spirits inhabiting the world possessed his or her own individual specific sound. The ancestral totem, for instance, seemed to posses an acoustic life and to respond to a certain sound. The imitation or simulation of the individual sound (or song) belonging to the totem enabled the man to identify himself with his

[1] Alfred Einstein, *A Short History of Music*, Cassell (1936), p. 1.
[2] Margaret Mead, *Sex and Temperament in Three Primitive Societies*, p. 247.

mystical ancestor and thus to maintain its life through the contact. Otherwise it would die.[1]

The ancestral totem was not the only being to possess his own sound and to be identified with it. Primitive man has often believed that every being, dead or alive, had his own secret sound or song to which he would respond and which might make him vulnerable to magic. For that reason he kept it secret from the sorcerers.[2] In a number of magic healing rites the medicine-man tried to discover the sound or song to which the sick man, or the spirit inhabiting him, would respond. This would give him contact with and power over the evil affecting the patient. The personal sound could often be connected with the timbre of the man's voice, which is a universally individual factor, and still observed today. Today a subconscious, personal secret sound seems to be present in some psychotic individuals, and may confirm the old belief that each man is born with his own inner sound to which he responds.

Primitive man identified himself with his surroundings when he imitated the sounds he heard, either vocally or on an instrument. Marius Schneider, who believes that 'vocal imitation is the strongest form of mystic participation in the surrounding world', states that it is not confined to the individual. He describes a mass experience in which the Aboriginals hold nature concerts. Each of the participants imitates a particular natural sound such as wind, rain, waves, trees or animals, the result of which is striking and magnificent.[3] Certain methods of musical education are trying today to revive these primitive customs.

The imitation of sound as a means of gaining power over its

[1] From Marius Schneider, 'Primitive Music', *New Oxford History of Music*, Vol. I, pp. I–12.
[2] Ibid.
[3] Marius Schneider, ibid., pp. 8, 9, 10.

original source is bound to the ancient Iso magic principle that 'like acts on like'—a principle applicable in music therapy. The magician endowed with such power could be the master of certain forces threatening man's safety or health. He had to know the formulas, rites, incantations and songs that would be protective or curative.

We may suppose that little by little the imitation of natural sounds became music, with a form and an expression of its own, and developed through various civilisations and cultures.

3. MUSIC, MAGIC AND RELIGION

Imitation and repetition are two processes through which man learns, develops and creates. They apply to sound when it becomes a verbal or musical language. We can observe and follow them in the infant going through the first steps of exploring and apprehending sound, as probably did our ancestors.

Organised sound which carries meaning and expression need not lose completely its mysterious character when it becomes symbolic and expresses a human emotion or a thought. When man created music he still believed it to be of supernatural origin and not man-made. Combarieu states that 'in all known civilisations music has been believed to have a divine origin. Everywhere it has been considered not as a creation of man, but as the work of a supernatural being. There is nothing similar in the history of art or drawing. Naturally, man has given to music itself the power he attributed to the gods.'[1] According to him the use of magic songs is one of the most ancient facts in the history of man and has a unique importance in the history of civilisation.[2]

Because of the impalpable and immaterial nature of sound, music is easily related to communication with the supernatural,

[1] J. Combarieu, *La Musique et la Magie*, p. 113.
[2] Ibid., p. 14.

MT—B

invisible world. Man perhaps has felt that he could himself partake of its divine quality when he used it himself. Jacques Chailley goes as far as suggesting that 'perhaps music is the only particle of the divine essence that man has been able to capture. . . . Music has enabled man to identify himself with the gods. . . . The gods have spoken to man, and man to the gods through music.'[1]

If our conceptions of man, religion or society have undergone many changes throughout history, certain beliefs or attitudes have remained strangely unchanged. The idea that there is something divine in music can still be found today. Throughout the ages the composer or the performer has often been thought to be divinely inspired, perhaps because such inspiration cannot be rationally explained. The thought can be followed from ancient times: Orpheus was the divinely inspired lyre player whose melodies could tame wild beasts and the dark powers of the underworld.

Even when the belief in the divine origin of music had become a thing of the past, the vocabulary used metaphorically to describe the nature or the effect of a musical experience was often related to the old belief. In his serious, rational book, Hector Chomet speaks of music as 'a divine emanation'.[2] More recently a music critic described a secular piece of music for soprano and tenor as 'magical' and stated that the performance of the singers sounded like 'immediate God-given inspiration'.[3]

4. MUSIC AND THE DEVIL

If music has sometimes been considered as a gift to man, coming from God and returning to Him, a gift which would contribute

---

[1] Jacques Chailley, *40,000 Years of Music*, Macdonald & Co., p. 54.
[2] Hector Chomet, *The Influence of Music on Health and Life*, translated from the French by Mrs Laura A. Flint, New York (1875).
[3] *The Times*, London, 2 September 1964.

to man's happiness and health, there was side by side another belief, that music could be used by Satan, like all other divine gifts. Man has often believed that music might help evil spirits to entice man to his spiritual or corporeal perdition. Long before the Christian era we find this expressed in ageless legends. For instance, the German story of the Lorelei whose songs provoked an irresistible melancholy and led men to drown in the Rhine— or Odysseus telling of the songs of the sirens which cast a spell on the sailors who could not resist their appeal and were wrecked on the rocks. The legend of the Pied Piper is well known all over Europe. In the little rat-infested town of Hamelin a strange man appeared from nowhere and offered to purge the town of its pests. He played on a flute an irresistible tune, the rats appeared from everywhere, followed him into the river in which he waded and were drowned. When the ungrateful inhabitants refused to pay him for his services he said nothing. But he started playing again, an even more enticing tune, and walked towards the river. All the children of the town followed him, hypnotised by the music, and they disappeared with him, never to be seen again.

The early Christian Church knew very well that music was not only a spiritual, elevating experience, but that it could also be evil because of its roots in pagan rites. The Christian Fathers tried to stamp out of music all traces of its pagan influence and to give music a spiritually curative virtue. But many early documents prove that music went on, taking part in the dark work of Satan. Some of them are very picturesque. A fourteenth-century text quoted by Alec Robertson speaks of the disorder and confusion that occasionally took place in the best-regulated churches and which were ascribed to 'the intervention of demons who were constantly striving to attack the monks on their weak side . . . and endeavouring by confusing singers to interrupt such psalms as "Domine quid multiplicati sunt" . . . and when a silly young monk almost at the bottom of a choir, annoyed by a psalm being pitched low, raised the key by a fifth, his indiscipline was attributed to one of those same demons.'[1]

Luther was an accomplished musician who looked at music as a true gift of God. Nevertheless he was well aware that Satan could use the divine gift towards his own evil ends. Luther tried to make music more appealing to his congregation by 'christianising' popular tunes and weeding out their pagan associations. He is even supposed to have said: 'Must the Devil have all the good tunes?'[2]

In the Middle Ages and as late as the eighteenth century some people still believed in Satan, witches and fairies living among them, whose evil work was often associated with music. Some trials of French and Scottish witches prove that music was an integral part of their gatherings. The Devil invented ribald songs and was the usual performer, but other members of the society could also supply the music. Pipes were in general use, also trumps and jew's harps. At Tranent in 1659 eight women and a man called John Douglas confessed to having many meetings with Satan, enlivened with music and dancing.[3] We find a vivid description of such a scene in Burns's *Alloway's Auld Haunted Kirk:*

> At Winnock bunken in the East [Ayr]
> Then sat Old Nick, in shape of beast;
> A towzie tyke, black, grim and large
> To gie them music was his charge.[4]

Pacts with the Devil in which music played the major part were believed to have occurred more recently and even in more

[1] Alec Robertson, 'Plainsong', *Pelican History of Music*, p. 195.
[2] *New Oxford History of Music*, Vol. II, p. 380.
[3] W. H. Hambley, *Tribal Dancing and Social Development*, H. F. & G. Witherby, London (1926).
[4] Ibid. (quoted by Hambley).

civilised parts of the world. The well-known story of Tartini's Devil's Sonata is worth recalling here, in the words of a French traveller of the eighteenth century:

'One night I dreamt that I had made a pact with the Devil for my soul. Everything went to my command; my novel servant (the Devil) anticipated every one of my wishes. Then the idea suggested itself to me to hand him my violin and to see what he would do with it. Great was my astonishment when I heard him play with consummate skill a sonata of such exquisite beauty as surpassed the boldest flights of my imagination. I felt enraptured, transported, enchanted, my breath failed me and—I awoke. Seizing my violin I tried to reproduce the sounds I had just heard. But in vain. The piece I then composed, the Devil's Sonata, although the best I ever wrote, how far was it below the one I had heard in my dream!'[1] This happened around 1720, when Tartini was about thirty years old. Today, the Devil's Sonata is a favourite piece in the violinist's repertoire, but it has lost its connection with the Devil.

It is possible that the violin could then lend itself easily to feats which had nothing divine or spiritual. In the nineteenth century Paganini's uncanny virtuosity was supposed to be of a devilish, certainly not a divine, nature. His bewildering technique aroused a great amount of suspicion which he took great care to cultivate by his behaviour and his appearance, that even suggested he might have a cloven hoof. He also seems to have had the power, as some popular performers of today, to mesmerise his audiences by his mere presence as well as by his playing, and delirious crowds followed him everywhere.[2]

For good, or for what was supposed to be evil, man has looked at music as a means of communication with the invisible world. Its mysterious and supernatural nature gave music the

[1] Quoted in *Grove's Dictionary of Music and Musicians*, Vol. 5, p. 268.
[2] R. Saussine, *Paganini*, Hutchinson, 1953, pp. 114–18.

power to heal or to harm, to spiritualise emotions or to provoke instinctive urges.

In spite of many ancient beliefs on the origin of music, we may now turn briefly to a scientific opinion which is of interest to our subject.

5. BIOLOGICAL ORIGIN OF MUSIC

Darwin's elaborate study of the origin of music is based on his theory of evolution. He discusses the incidence and significance of expressive sounds produced by all species of animals, especially of birds whose voices can express various emotions such as distress, fear, anger, triumph or mere happiness. He noticed the fact that the true songs of most birds served as a charm or as a call note to the other sex.[1] Other naturalists thought that birds sang for other purposes, to express rivalry or emulation.[2] Darwin also found that certain birds can discriminate between different levels of musical achievement, that the female canary or the female finch would always choose the best singer for her mate.

Darwin came to the conclusion that 'from the deeply laid principle of inherited association musical tone (in this case) would be likely to call up vaguely and indefinitely the strong emotions of a long past age'.[3] He also made the following remark of special interest to us:

'The impassionate orator, bard or musician, when with his varied tones and cadences he excites the strongest emotions in his hearers, little suspects that he uses the same means by which his half-human ancestors long ago aroused each other's ardent passions during their courtship and rivalry.'[4]

The musical achievement of birds is functional and aims at

---

[1] Charles Darwin, *The Descent of Man*, J. Murray (1909), p. 565.
[2] Ibid., p. 565.
[3] Ibid.
[4] Ibid., p. 873.

the propagation of the species. Darwin was puzzled by the fact that man had continued to indulge in a seemingly senseless activity which could not be explained scientifically. He stated that 'as neither the enjoyment of music nor the capacity of producing musical notes are faculties of the least use to man in reference to his daily habits of life, they must be ranked among the most mysterious with which he is endowed',[1] to which remark William Wallace replied that 'the insistence upon *utility* by men of science is fatal to any hypothesis regarding music'.[2]

Both of them were completely mistaken with regard to the historical uses of music. Music for a long time was purely functional and not used for its own sake.

If the sounds made by animals, especially birds, had been instrumental in the emergence of music, man in turn has been interested in the responses of animals to music. A number of studies have been made, from the eighteenth century onwards, which were mostly speculative, but prove man's insatiable curiosity about the effect of music on body and mind. Today, these studies take a renewed interest through the various psychological experiments on the behaviour and the conditioning of animals. Pavlov's dog responded to the sound of a bell, as even infants may respond to the chime bells of the ice-cream man, sounds related to an anticipated and gustative pleasure. Although animals do not seem to respond to rhythm, for which the hearer must be able to apprehend a pattern of organised sounds, the colour of the tone and its frequency and intensity together with the continuity of the music in time make definite impressions on some animals. These impressions do not require a high intelligence process to be felt. Sometimes the mere vibration of a sound can attract a spider or a snake. It is said that cows yield more

[1] Ibid., p. 867.
[2] William Wallace, *The Threshold of Music*, MacMillan & Co. (1908), p. 7.

milk when background music is being played. We propose to discuss these facts in the following chapter.

6. MUSICAL INSTRUMENTS

Certain musical instruments in primitive times were supposed to possess magical power, to be inhabited by or to symbolise a supernatural being. In some countries drums were believed to be of magic origin, sacrifices were made to them, and they were even offered food. Maracas were identified with the head of a supernatural being.[1]

As we have seen, the soul of the totemic ancestor was supposed to be present in the bull roarer of the Australian tribes. The material from which the instrument was made, such as bone or wood, was still connected with its former origin and could act on man, animal or vegetable from which it came. The shape of the instrument, or its tone, often had sexual connotations. Some instruments were used specifically in healing rites, sometimes as a kind of medical apparatus. In some parts of Africa the witch doctor still uses a magic drum and an *ouombi* harp to play over the stomach of the patient.[2]

The musical instruments used by the magician during certain rites were a symbol of his power. He often wore rattles which added to the effect of his gesticulations and of his attire.

The Greek mythology tells of a number of musical instruments invented, played and given to man by the gods. The flute—or aulos—was Athanea's gift; Pan played the harmonica; Apollo had made the lyre out of a tortoise shell. It was the favourite instrument of the Greek gods.

Musical instruments are concrete, positive objects that man can make, improve or transform. Unlike music, many of them

---

[1] Klaus P. Waschmann, *Musical Instruments through the Ages*, ed. by A. Baines, Pelican Books, pp. 33, 36.
[2] Jacques Chailley, *40,000 Years of Music*, p. 59.

rapidly lost their association with the supernatural world. But some of them still possess a certain fascination and make a mysterious appeal to children, who live in an animistic world where objects have an inner life of their own. The primitive or modern player has always identified himself with his instrument, which is a prolongation of his body and transforms into sound his psychomotor impulses and liberates them. The manipulation of an instrument demands also conscious control of movement in time and space, and obedience to certain laws of acoustics. The process has a well-known therapeutic value.

II
Music in Healing

MAN has always considered illness as an abnormal state. He has explained its causes and has applied remedies including music in the light of his actual knowledge and beliefs. Although his concept of illness and his attitude towards healing have changed continually throughout the centuries, man's reactions to musical experiences have remained basically unchanged. The effects of music on the sick man's mind and body have kept a remarkable similarity since time immemorial. The study of music as a therapeutic means can follow a consistent thread based on the development of medical treatment itself. We propose to take a chronological approach in this chapter and divide into three headings a brief survey of healing processes—those related to magic, to religion, to rational thought—processes to which music has been applied according to the beliefs and customs of the time.

Moreover, the function and the personality of the healer produced a healer-patient relationship which at all times has played an important part in the result of the treatment.

The healer using music has been in turn through the ages a magician—a priest—a physician or a music specialist. Ultimately, and in any kind of society, the sick man seeking cure and relief finds himself in the hands of the man who possesses some power over the cause of his illness. At all times their relationship has been based on the willingness of the patient to submit to the treatment and on his responses to the treatment given by the healer. There must be a mutual confidence in the prescribed method, especially when fear intervenes or when a risk has to be taken. The personality of the healer and the part he plays in the life of the community have a considerable influence on the patient's favourable or adverse response to the treatment.

From the Ebers papers we gather that there were already in Egypt in the fifteenth century B.C. three types of healers: the exorcist or magician, the priest and the physician,[1] whom we meet in all forms of civilisation under different names. We also find throughout history a number of musicians called to act as therapists, such as the ancient Egyptian musician-priestess Shebut-n-mut,[2] or David the harp player of the Bible, or the Greek lyre player Thimoteus,[3] or the Arab Al Farabi,[4] the Italian eighteenth-century singer Farinelli—and all the anonymous musicians who were engaged to play to the sufferers of Tarantism—and many others in modern times.

All these healers, magicians, priests, physicians or musicians had a different kind of relationship with the patients. Their use of music in healing varied according to their conception of illness and its treatment, to their function and beliefs, and very much to their musical skill and knowledge.

7. MUSIC IN MAGICAL HEALING

Primitive man believed that the universe was magical and ruled by spirits or supernatural forces whose manifestations were mostly evil or threatening and with whom he had to come to terms. He tried to protect himself and to control or dominate the supernatural world or the forces of nature through magic. The

---

[1] Henry E. Sigerist, *Civilization and Disease*, Phoenix Books, University of Chicago Press (1962), p. 133.

[2] Papyrus Hent Tani, British Museum.

[3] Hector Chomet, *The Influence of Music on Health and Life*, p. 195.

[4] J. Combarieu, *La Musique et la Magie*, p. 94.

attempt to dominate natural forces through magical means has persisted through the centuries in spite of the advances in scientific knowledge. We can still find some manifestations of it in our rational world, where superstitions and beliefs in magic in some form do exist.

Primitive man living in a world of spirits and magic logically believed that illness was due to magical causes and that it needed magical remedies. He thought that sickness was caused by the possession of an evil spirit that had to be cast out. The magician, medicine man or *shaman* was supposed to know the secret magic formulas which controlled the evil spirits. He used orders, threats, cajolations, sometimes even deceit during special and complex healing ceremonies aiming at coercing the spirit. Music, rhythms, songs and dances played a vital part in magic healing rites which were secret, either individual or shared by the whole community. Sound and music, being of magic origin, were used to communicate directly with the spirit. Their magical property could help to penetrate and to break up the resistance of the spirit of disease.

Since primitive man never realised that illness was the result of some pathological disorder, the curative means he used were directed not at the patient but through him at the evil spirit from which he had to be liberated. The means were deliberately shrouded in mystery, which added to the authority of the magician. Healing rites put the patient at the mercy of the healer, his body and his soul were the passive seat of the fight between the magician and the evil spirit possessing him—a fight that often terrified the sick man, since nothing was done to reassure him, no pity or compassion was shown to him in tribal life.

Certain natural means such as herbs, earth or water were supposed to be curative only because the spirit inhabiting them could fight the evil spirit. Moreover, most of them were effective only if the magician used them with the proper song or incantation, of which he was the sole possessor.

Some of the magical healing means possessed a curative value which we recognize today on scientific grounds. We use today some of the same medicinal plants for their chemical value, but without the incantations or songs which were indispensable in primitive medicine. Certain healing rites, especially when used with music, must have produced on the sick man powerful physiological or psychological effects or catharsis, and induced certain states medically desirable or harmful. Although the music was not meant to affect the patient himself, he must have been in a receptive and vulnerable state and could not help being influenced directly by the sounds of music and rhythms which connected him with the invisible world.

The magician was not concerned with this; he used music solely as a means of communication with and of domination over the spirit of illness. The music expressed his unyielding will-power through the endless monotony of the rhythm. His songs carried words of persuasion or threat on a melody that grew softer or louder, slower or faster, according to the mood and to the response of the spirit.

Music was not usually the main element in the rites, but it helped to integrate dynamically almost all stages of a ceremonial which brought into action many symbols of the elemental forces surrounding man, such as water, earth, fire and the vegetable and animal kingdoms.

8. MAGICIAN-PATIENT RELATIONSHIP

The personality of the magician and his social position in the tribe gave a particular character to his relationship with the sick man. First, the magician was in every way an unusual kind of being. Paul Radin presumes that he was probably a unique and isolated being who set a high value on the necessity for solitude for acquiring wisdom and on the educative effects of suffering. He must have been a maladjusted individual who could think for himself and not collectively and was not taking part in the searching for food or communal life.[1]

Since the magician possessed the necessary magical knowledge, he might have been highly regarded, but, because of his power, he was mostly feared, and might even have been hated. Schneider sees him as a man 'who is honoured in public, but avoided in private. That he is able to traffic with the world of spirits makes him a somewhat sinister figure, and the more intensely a community feels his power, the more it tries to keep him at arm's length. Since it also needs him, it cannot banish him completely; so it acknowledges him secretly or openly, yet rejects him because it cannot forgive him his superior powers.'[2] His opinion is shared by a number of anthropologists.

The personality and the function of the magician prevented him from mixing with the daily life of the tribe, except as an intermediary between man and the spirits or the deities that had to be appeased or coerced, flattered or threatened. Even if the secret knowledge he possessed brought fear and suspicion, the magician was entrusted to deal with man's complete cycle of tribal life, birth and death, in health and in illness, war and peace, and to conduct all the ceremonies vital to the community. He was indispensable but not loved, feared more than respected, and lived apart from ordinary daily life. When he was called to cure a sick man there was no sympathy, friendship or affection between him and the patient. The music he used was not meant to alleviate the pain or to give pleasure. It was entirely directed at the evil spirit who could be influenced by incantations, songs, rhythms or by the sound of certain musical instruments.

[1] Paul Radin, *Music and Medicine*, ed. Schuman, New York.
[2] Marius Schneider, 'Primitive Music', *New Oxford History of Music*, Vol. I, p. 41.

The attitude of the patient towards the magician must have been mostly one of fear. There was little hope for the infirm or the sick in tribal life. Most tribes rejected those for whom it had no use, although they often respected the old, the elders who possessed the wisdom and experience given by a long life.

But even if the patient was fearful, and the magician indifferent to the individual, both shared the belief or hope that the healing rites could bring cure or relief. Possibly there were in primitive as well as at all times healers who exploited the distress and needs of the sick man. But basically, the magician believed in the effectiveness of his art. His magic embodied the primitive man's conception of the world around him. In his own way, the magician acted logically and with confidence. His music must have been convincing. Combarieu suggests that when he undertook a cure he was just as sincere and convinced as a modern scientist in his laboratory.[1] Moreover, he was certain that without songs, music or incantations some of his remedies could not work.

Very little is known about the initiation or training a magician had to undergo in order to acquire his power, and it would be wrong to generalise the data that is obtainable. But from many observations made in different countries, we may deduce that the magician must have possessed some psychic characteristics such as the ability to go into a trance, to have visions or to hypnotise people. Perhaps he was mentally unstable. He was certainly very sensitive to sound and music.

The type of neophyte chosen to become a magician in the primitive parts of Siberia has been described by Hambley: 'A boy of neurotic temperament who is subject to fits of hysteria is selected for training which consists of fastings, ceremonials and seclusion in the loneliest mountain ravines. Such a course naturally emphasises physical weakness and mental abnormality until at last the youth is in such a highly sensitive state that

[1] J. Combarieu, *La Musique et la Magie*, p. 18.

hysteria followed by trance can be self-induced by violent dancing, singing and drum beating.'[1] There were among the American Indians secret societies of magicians in which novices were admitted after special initiation ceremonies.[2]

But we know little about the way they acquired their knowledge of curative means; many of them were secret and handed on. We hear that in the Indian tribes of Ontario and Red River certain individuals were at the same time magicians, priests, prophets and music teachers. They possessed great knowledge of the curative virtue of plants and roots, but these had to be used only with the special incantation or song which made them effective. The neophyte learnt how to prepare his songs as well as his concoctions, and he also invented new musical and vegetal formulas. His own songs were the speciality which gave him his power, they belonged to him and no one else dared to use them.[3]

Certain curative songs were said to come from supernatural sources in dreams or visions. The owner of the song was the man to whom it had been revealed with the instructions for procedure and the knowledge of the herbs used. These were kept secret.[4]

We know scarcely anything about the origin of the music used in primitive healing rites, although some anthropologists have collected a number of healing tunes and their words. Much of the most primitive ones must have been imitative when man tried to evoke through sound the threatening forces surrounding him.

In spite of the monotony of the music, its performance went

[1] W. D. Hambley, *Tribal Dancing and Social Development*, pp. 248–9.
[2] Ibid., p. 249.
[3] J. Combarieu, *La Musique et la Magie*, collected from B. J. Hofman, 17th Annual Report of Ethnology, Washington Government Printing Office.
[4] Frances Desmore, 'The Use of Music by American Indians' (1891), p. 25 etc., in *Music and Medicine*, ed. by Schullian and Schoen, Henry Schuman Inc., New York (1948).

through different emotional moods, since it tried to persuade, flatter, cajole or threaten the evil spirit. Certain songs were used for specific illnesses. Various anthropologists at different times have collected primitive songs in America, Africa and Europe,[1] and a number of them are medicine music. We find among these a few of a slow character with long sustained notes. But most of the medicine songs we have seen are rapid (over 100 beats per minute), rhythmical and repetitive. A few include a drum accompaniment.

The feeling of awe and fear towards those who possess magical power or communicate with evil forces has persisted throughout history. It created utter dependence of the sick man under the domination of the magician. All the musical means he used, such as incantations, rhythms, songs, added greatly to the atmosphere of mystery and secrecy surrounding the healer. Moreover, the ignorance and dependence in which the patient found himself increased his fear. This feeling has been natural to all patients and we can still observe it today. But today music is used to allay fear and dispel anxiety in the patient. The magician's therapy had nothing to do with human relationship or compassion, it was a communication with the world of spirits.

In religious healing, music was still used as a means of communication with the supernatural world, but it was based on a completely different conception of the relationship created by an illness.

9. MUSIC IN RELIGIOUS HEALING
In the Ancient World
The primitive belief that illness was caused by the possession of an evil spirit persisted throughout the ancient world, especially with regard to mental disorder. But at the same time man's conception of illness took a different form. He slowly acquired the

[1] Those collected in Asia are not included in this study. See p. 12.

MT—C

idea that disease was a pathological state, even when he still believed that its occurrence was due to supernatural influences. He thought that it had been sent by an angry god, in punishment for a sin or a transgression of a rule, whether conscious or unconscious. It was imperative to find out first not the physiological cause of the illness but the nature of the fault of which the patient was guilty. He had to appease the gods and to atone before he could be cured.

The ancient gods were not elemental spirits to be dominated by magic—they were deities created in man's image. They possessed man's attributes and behaved rather like supernatural rulers or kings, expecting offerings and retributions. They also took an active part in man's public and private life, presided over his specific needs and activities such as war and peace, or medicine, or music.

Isis and Serapis in ancient Egypt were the great healers, and the Greek Apollo was the god of music as well as the god of medicine. Men supreme in their field were often deified after their death. The Egyptians made a god of their physician Imhotep, as the Greeks deified Aesculapius and Orpheus the great musician.[1]

Illness and the breaking of the law were closely connected in the ancient world. The familiar rites of purification in which music was sometimes used linked together physical and spiritual healing.

The belief that illness was sent by a revengeful god who had to be appeased before the sick man could recover his health did not rule out a rational approach to physical illness, and this will be discussed in the next chapter. Mental illness, on the whole, was still attributed to the possession of an evil spirit which had to be cast out before the patient could recover his sanity. Certain

[1] C. Singer, *Short History of Medicine*, Clarendon Press, Oxford (1928), p. 7.

deities were responsible for the loss of reason, such as the Furies who drove man to madness and often to his physical and spiritual perdition.

Even when a medical treatment was available no cure of illness could be effected without propitiating the gods from whom man hoped to get a human response of justice or compassion. The sick man approached the gods in order to appease those whose power he had no means to transcend or to coerce. He took a respectful and humble attitude, offered prayers, supplications, promises, gifts and even sometimes barter. He addressed them usually through the priest, who knew all the formulas, to the specific deity he thought he had offended, or to a god who possessed the power to heal.

Among these was the most famous healer of the antique world, Aesculapius, who came from a medical family and was deified after his death. His temples, including the famous one in Epidaurus, were places of worship as well as healing shrines, just as is Lourdes today. We find in these temples of healing many tablets recording miraculous cures from patients, some of whom had tried in vain to be cured by the available medical means of the day. In these Greek temples were hymn specialists called aretalogists, among others, who attended the patients during the mysteries of incubation.

Apollo, the god of medicine, was often invoked in cases of illness, but since he also presided over music he had given man certain musical means through which they could address him, such as the lyre on which he performed himself. It is interesting to note that Apollo as god of music possessed one of the characteristics of some human performers, namely vanity. He was so jealous of his musical skill that he was supposed to have skinned alive the satyr Marsyas, who had dared to dispute with him the prize of music. He gave asses' ears to King Midas, who had preferred Pan's pipes to the lyre. It was important, therefore, when singing or playing to Apollo to choose music that would flatter him agreeably.

The great and touching legend of Orpheus shows the power that the Greeks attributed to music over the natural and the supernatural world. Since music and even musical instruments were believed to be a gift from the gods, the Greeks used it to address the gods and to propitiate them, hoping that it would reach them and that they would respond.

Music, then, had become a means of human personal communication with the deity. It was no more a threatening means to force or dominate supernatural forces. Man used it as an instrument of persuasion which had to be pleasing to a deity who like man was sensitive to harmony and beauty. The music accompanying antique healing rites and addressed to the god must have even indirectly put the patient in a relaxed, hopeful and receptive mood. Ceremonies were conducted by the priests; the ritual incantations, songs or music were provided by the priest himself or by specialists attached to the temple.

The orgies and other well-known pagan rites that included dances and much music had no direct healing purposes. But they provided a tremendous physical and psychological outlet that cannot be ignored in a study of therapeutic musical means. The incidence of Tarantism in Europe in the Middle Ages and its cure through frenzied music and dances has sometimes been interpreted as a revival of pagan orgies. Music, then, was used with deliberate healing purposes, as we will discuss in the course of our study.

The personality of the priest and the functions he had to fulfil in the antique world are of interest to our study, because he was responsible for all religious rites that affected public life, including health and illness. He knew all the formulas through which the gods could be approached and reached. These formulas were extremely complicated, ancient and secret, and jealously guarded by the priests.

In the course of the centuries the priest had succeeded the father as the head of the community that had sprung out of the family unit. He was a kind of father-figure chosen by the gods themselves, first through heredity, later on by the casting of lots which expressed the will of the gods. His person, therefore, was agreeable to them. The priest was a sacred person, trusted by the community, but not loved. Unlike the magician, he lived openly among his people. His private and public life was outwardly at least respectable.[1] For a long time he was magistrate as well as priest, in charge of justice and religion, whose laws were inseparable.

His functions were based on traditions that went back to time immemorial when the father-priest, head of the family, knew all the religious formulas linked with ancestral worship. These formulas had first been passed from mouth to mouth and then had been inscribed in a book. They consisted in hymns, or songs that had to be sung with the exact rhythm, the order of which had to be scrupulously followed—any change or mistake was an act of impiety severely punished by the State since it displeased the gods and imperilled the safety of the whole community.[2]

The same author tells us that these religious formulas and songs had been tried in the past and their use had been effective, therefore agreeable to the gods. Some of the sacred books contained collections of songs and hymns sometimes so ancient that nobody understood the language any more, although people went on singing them and believing in their efficacity.[3]

The priest acquired his knowledge through the books that were kept secret. He had to know all the details concerning the sacred rites, including those against illnesses and epidemics; he

[1] Fustel de Coulanges, The Ancient City, p. 183.
[2] Ibid., p. 169.
[3] Ibid., p. 169.

had to please the deity, otherwise the god might be antagonised and provoke disaster.

Instrumental and choral music was used during the ceremonies, according to a ritual suitable to the occasion. The priest sang during the ceremonies, but does not seem to have played a musical instrument. This probably was left to his personal band of flautists who played during the sacrifices over which he officiated. There were also the cantors or choir who sang during the ceremonies.[1]

The priest, as well as the magician, was the link between the defenceless patient and the supreme power. Both were in charge of the healing rites, and their intervention was in some way indirect. But the priest's function was different. His duty consisted in making the gods reveal the cause of the illness, indicate the remedy that would cure it or demand the sacrifice that would appease them.

When the priest used music as a means of communication with the gods it was solely to be agreeable to them and gain their goodwill. It was not supposed to be an emotional experience through which the patient and the priest could relate to one another and create some kind of human contact. There was no love between the supplicant and the gods or their intermediary.

In the Christian Era

The belief that disease may be cured through divine intervention is part of a religious faith; it has persisted throughout the centuries up to our time. In the Christian era the pagan gods specially concerned with health and sickness had disappeared, but they were then replaced by a legion of saints to be invoked in certain cases of illness: for instance, St Sebastian for the plague; St Lazarus for leprosy; St Vitus for epilepsy; St Blaisey for throat diseases, and many others. Hymns and music carried

[1] Glotz, *The Greek City*, Kegan Paul (1929), p. 221.

the patient's supplications for help and healing. This did not preclude the patient from seeking the available medical treatment, but he probably made sure of both worlds, as he sometimes still does.

Christianity brought new ethical concepts, unknown to the primitive and the ancient world, of a loving God, of compassion and charity towards the weak, the sick and the poor. Its attitude towards disease was one of humility and holy obedience to suffering which could help man to gain eternal bliss.

After the fall of the Roman Empire and during the Dark Ages, the practice of medicine disappeared from western Europe. It was kept smouldering by the religious orders, who gave shelter and some medical care to the sick and the poor. They founded the first hospitals at the time of the Crusades. The humanitarian attitude of the monks towards the sick confirmed the belief that the man of God was also the man who could fight illness, and he did so sometimes through medical means as well as prayers.

Nevertheless the man of God saw in the patient a body meant to perish sooner or later and an immortal soul to be saved. The relationship between the priest and the sick man was a humane and personal one in which the priest tried to bring the patient nearer to God and to ease his sufferings through divine or human intervention.

Although he was not directly concerned with physical illness when a physician was available, his ministry gave him an intimate knowledge of the problems of his flock and created a human relationship between him and the sufferer, a relationship of understanding and confidence. But too often the teaching of the Church produced in the patient a sense of sin and fear for the salvation of his soul after death and altered his relation with the priest.

Early in the Middle Ages the priests realised very well how

much music and art could influence man, for good or evil, even if he was not educated. The masterpieces in art and music commissioned by the Church to adorn the cathedrals and enhance the effect of the services were not solely offerings to the glory of God: they were also meant to bring the faithful nearer to God through the beauty and expression of sounds and pictures, to put them in a receptive and spiritual mood. The priest himself was sensitive to such influences and shared them with his congregation. Some of them were fine musicians or artists. Saint Bernard de Clairvaux (1090–1153) gives these directions to his monks: 'Let the chant be full of gravity . . . let it be sweet, yet without levity, and while it pleases the ear let it move the heart. It should alleviate sadness and calm the angry spirit.'[1]

Throughout the whole history of Christianity and under holy and saintly patronage shrines continued to flourish everywhere where believers could seek cures or relief from disease. In most of them music was and is still today an indispensable element in the ritual, the liturgy and the processions in which the faithful participated. Music, then, as it always is, was part of a collective religious experience that affected every one of the participants. This can be observed in Lourdes today, as in other similar shrines.

The power to heal in the Middle Ages was not confined to God or to His saints. From the eleventh century the kings of England and France were supposed to possess by divine right the power to cure certain diseases by the laying on of hands, a ritual that did not include music.

It is not surprising that as late as the sixteenth century the famous surgeon Ambroise Paré used to conclude his case records with these words: 'Je le pansay et Dieu le guarist' (I dressed him

[1] St Bernard de Clairvaux (1090–1153) in a direction to his monks. Quoted by Alec Robertson, 'Plainsong', *Pelican History of Music*, p. 195.

and God healed him).[1] Although he possessed a fine scientific mind much in advance of his time, Ambroise Paré believed that medical treatment, however skilful, was not enough to cure illness and that the physician could not succeed without some kind of divine help. He certainly believed also in the therapeutic virtue of aesthetic pleasure, since he advocated the use of music in convalescence.

In Christian as well as in pagan times man has turned towards supernatural powers for help or comfort in cases of sickness or need, irrespective of his belief in the available medical treatment. But in the course of time his attitude towards divine help underwent great changes related to the growth of his consciousness as an individual. Since the Christian was concerned with the salvation of his own personal soul for eternal life, his relationship with God became a personal, intimate one. At the same time, as he was seeking for means of self-expression, music became to him a personal experience carrying human emotions. Man spoke to man through his music as he had spoken to God.

Thus man became aware of the power of music over his own psychological and spiritual state, since it could arouse the best in him, harmonise and purify his emotions, and even sublimate his instinctive urges. Religious healing at all times has called forth spiritual forces within and without man in order to fight evil, ills and suffering. Among them, music may be considered as a spiritual experience overriding for a time the feeling of pain or anxiety, and thus bringing relief.

Moreover, to many of the believers in spiritual healing, music seems to carry a divine message of hope and redemption, perhaps still linked with the ancient belief in its divine essence.

The gratitude towards God of a patient cured of a severe illness has often been expressed in a gift, or even sometimes in

[1] D. W. Singer, *Ambroise Paré*, John Bale Sons & Danielsson Ltd. (1924), p. 38.

music, the most immaterial of all thanksgiving. Beethoven wrote some of his most moving pages to thank God for his return to health after a grave illness. There his music was more than coming 'from the heart and going to the heart'; it was coming from the heart and going to God, the healer.

10. MUSIC IN RATIONAL HEALING

In Antiquity

Babylon and ancient Egypt saw the birth of a rational attitude to illness. It grew further in ancient Greece, took root and from there went to Rome. The Greeks were the first to possess what Charles Singer calls a 'scientific consciousness' which more or less disappeared with their civilisation. 'For thousands of years that followed the break-up of the Roman Empire the medical practice in Europe was at its best a corrupted imitation and misunderstanding of the Hippocratic teaching; at worst it descended to a low level of animism and magic.'[1]

Side by side with magical or religious customs we find in ancient Greece many of our modern ideas on health and disease not connected with magic or religion, but rational and scientific as well as philosphical and ethical. Since Greek thought integrated the known disciplines of the day such as mathematics, philosophy, medicine and music, Greek concepts have a unique place in the history of music therapy. The fact that Apollo presided over music and medicine may be symbolic of the interrelation of the two disciplines.

The Greeks tried to find reason and intellectual logic in the world around them and in man himself. Man to them was not only part of but the centre of a universal harmony. Their ideal was to attain perfect harmony between body and soul, between habits and reason, between intellect and emotions. Man could

[1] Charles Singer, *Short History of Medicine*, Clarendon Press, Oxford (1928), pp. 15–16.

then become the master of himself. The balance between body and soul was health, a thought expressed by Juvenal in his famous maxim: *Mens sana in corpore sano*. Greek philosophers considered illness as a disorder in the strict sense of the word. The order between body and soul was disturbed and had to be restored. It was the duty of the State to protect and to promote harmony by every means capable of creating health and order, and to fight against any form of disorder including illness.

A rational cure can take place only when the illness has been observed and diagnosed and when a logical remedy is found and can be applied. Even if Greek medicine was still empirical and subjective and had not been able to supersede magic or religious healing, the Greek physicians knew how to observe carefully the symptoms of disease. Some of their descriptions of illness, including mental disorder, are clinically quite accurate.

The Greek psychosomatic conception of illness explains why music, which is order and harmony affecting the whole man, played such an important part in the Greek approach to the problems of health. Music was an integral part of Greek life. The philosophers carried out profound investigations on its ethics and character, on its effects on soul and body. They drew conclusions on the therapeutic value of music.

The Greeks applied music systematically as a curative or preventive means that could and should be controlled, since its effects on man's physical and mental state were predictable. They went as far as to say that the use of music should be controlled by the State.

If Hippocrates is called the father of medicine, we may recognise Plato and Aristotle as the forerunners of music therapy, which is the controlled use of music. Aristotle gives music a definite medical value when he says that people who suffer from uncontrollable emotions, 'after listening to melodies which raise the soul to ecstasy relapse to their normal condition as if they had experienced a medical or purgative treatment'.[1]

The Greek analysis of the effect of music went very deep. According to Aristotle, Socrates spoke of the delayed action of intoxicating music. He was supposed to have regarded the lax harmonies 'as intoxicating, not in reference of intoxicating at the time—for it rather produces a disposition to revelry, but an intoxication when the actual fit has passed away'.[2]

The cathartic purge of the emotions was an important process towards mental health in Greek life, usually through dramatic or musical performances. Aesclepius, a famous physician, is said to have prescribed music and harmony for emotionally disturbed people.[3]

The Greeks analysed music and its elements. Their theories are generally related to modes or sequences of notes which carried a mathematical meaning. Pythagoras, the mathematician-physician, is said to have used music with mental patients which he called 'musical medicine'. He had developed a 'mystique' of numerology which he expressed in musical terms.[4] The musical emotion was provoked by certain combinations of sounds in the different modes or scales which were probably related to the tuning of the lyre, Apollo's gift to man. Unfortunately there is practically nothing left of Greek music. We know that it was mainly melodic, closely related to the rhythm of the language. Harmony as we understand it scarcely existed; the effect was produced by melodic intervals, by tone colour or rhythm, on which we can only speculate. Even if the melodic intervals contained in these scales can produce on our modern ears effects of

[1] Aristotle, *Politics*, Book V, Ch. VII, p. 256 [Macmillan & Co. (1888)].
[2] Ibid., Book V, Ch. VII, p. 248.
[3] Dr Stafford Clark, *Psychiatry Today*, Pelican Books, p. 22.
[4] Brian Powell, 'The Early Renaissance', *Pelican History of Music*, ed. by A. Robertson and D. Stevens, Vol. II (1963), p. 36.

tension or relaxation, we have no way of finding out what the music sounded like and why it produced the effects so carefully described in the writings of the time.

Certain modes were supposed to possess an ethical value, others an emotional one. Plato believed that the character of each mode produced specific effects on the morals of the listener—it is interesting to note that he seemed to attribute a lasting value to these effects. Aristotle in his *Politics* was less assertive than Plato, but he thought that as a means of education the ethical melodies and their corresponding harmonies should be employed in the development of character. He advocated, for instance, the use of the Dorian mode which had a spirit of valour; or the Lydian which was particularly suited to young children. He thought that Socrates was wrong in attributing ethical value to the Phrygian mode, since it was too strongly exciting and emotional.[1]

The following list drawn by another author, Cassiodorus, shows how detailed was the analysis of mode effects. His assessment was probably a personal one, although it reflects more or less other authors' opinions. In modern times there have been similar assessments on the effect of certain keys, most of them subjective.

> Dorian is related to modesty and purity.
> Phrygian stimulates to fierce combat.
> Aeolian composes mental disturbance, induces sleep.
> Ionian whets dull intellects, provokes desire for heavenly things.
> Lydian soothes the soul when oppressed with excessive care.[2]

Greek musical instruments belonged to two main families:

[1] Aristotle, *Politics*, Book V, Ch. VII, pp. 247–8.
[2] Bruno Meinecke, 'Classical Antiquity', *Music and Medicine*, ed. by Schoen and Schullian, Pub. Henry Schuman Inc., New York (1948), p. 69.

those with plucked strings, namely the lyre used for accompanying songs, and psalteries, and the wind instruments which could be played alone such as the *aulos* or the flute. We must remember that wind instruments were to the Greek the only tone-sustaining instruments which possessed the characteristics of the human voice. Hence their striking effects on the listeners of that time, whose ears were not conditioned to the intensity and dynamism of the violin. Already in primitive times the flute played in the high register had been used as particularly effective in sexual magic.[1] We find in Greek texts many references to the strong impact made by the flute on the emotions. It was believed to arouse passions and for that reason produce catharsis.

Aristotle expressed the opinion that the flute was an instrument of a strongly exciting rather than an ethical character and should consequently be employed only upon occasions when the object of the music is the purging of the emotions rather than the improvement of the mind.[2]

Plato had gone further and advocated the medical use of the flute against Korybantism.[3]

The use of the flute as a therapeutic means was followed up by the Arabs, who inherited many of the Greek traditions in medicine. They used it in their hospital wards for mental patients.

Some physicians in Antiquity thought that the peculiar sound vibrations produced by the flute could affect man's body, independently from the emotions. Democritus in a medical treatise on 'Deadly Infections' recommended the flute as medicine for many ills the flesh is heir to.[4]

---

[1] Marius Schneider, 'Primitive Music', *New Oxford History of Music*, p. 57.
[2] Aristotle, *Politics*, Book V, Ch. VI, p. 242.
[3] Plato, *Conviv.* 245E, quoted by J. Combarieu, *La Musique et la Magie*.
[4] H. E. Sigerist, *Civilisation and Disease*, p. 213.

The vibrations were also supposed to affect a diseased part, as in sciatica, and had the power 'to make the flesh palpitate and revive' when the musician played upon the body of the patient.[1]

The Greeks observed only a few purely physiological effects of music, for instance on insomnia. It is said that Meceana, who suffered from anxiety, recovered his sleep by the use of background music.[2] Suitable music, especially played on the zither, was recommended during meals to help the digestion.[3] On the other hand, some people objected to that custom and the poet Martial found himself fortunate if he was invited to dine without a piper to drown the conversation.[4]

Most of the observations taken by some authors at various times are on the effects of listening to music. Nevertheless, some amateur performers found in music-making an outlet for disturbing moods. Homer tells us that Agamemnon's ambassadors found Achilles sulking in his tent, but playing on a magnificent lyre and singing away his anger.

Aristotle advocated the use of musical rattles as an outlet for the energy of destructive children who would otherwise smash the furniture.[5] But on the whole the Greek concept of music therapy was through listening to rather than making music. Sigerist states that the process was 'a kind of psychotherapy that affected the body through the medium of the soul',[6] because 'when a disorder had developed the Greek physician tried to restore the lost balance physically with medicine, mentally with music. Medicine and music were thus drawn into the circle of their investigations.'[7]

[1] H. Chomet, *The Influence of Music on Health*.
[2] Bruno Meinecke, 'Classical Antiquity', *Music and Medicine*, p. 75.
[3] J. Combarieu, *La Musique et la Magie*, p. 292.
[4] From J. E. Scott, *New Oxford History of Music*, Vol. I, p. 413.
[5] Aristotle, *Politics*, Book V, Ch. VI, p. 240.
[6] H. E. Sigerist, *Civilisation and Disease*, p. 213.
[7] Ibid., p. 149.

A number of Greek physicians, as happens today, were sceptical or cautious about the value of music in medicine. Caelius Aurelianus wisely condemned the indiscriminate use of music. He had observed that 'in the treatment of madness certain physicians employ exciting music without any discretion which may provoke good effects when applied in the right way, but on the other hand may cause much harm in a number of cases',[1] and these words of wisdom are still applicable today. Already in the second century the physician Soramus seems to have suffered from the enthusiasm of the exponents of music therapy. He thought that 'people were stupid who believed that the violence of the disease could be driven out by melodies and a song'.[2]

The Greek concept of music in healing was neither magical nor religious. The Greeks applied their clinical and logical minds to its therapeutic use, which continued in Roman times. At the fall of the Roman Empire their scientific spirit sank into the Dark Ages, and with it a rational conception of music therapy. But as we have seen, music continued to be used in religious or magic healing and thus could still be of some use to the sick man.

From the Renaissance to the Twentieth Century

After the fall of the Roman Empire and during the Dark Ages the practice of medicine was kept alive in Alexandria and passed into the hands of the Arabs in the countries they occupied in southern Europe. Many Greek medical texts were buried in European monasteries for several centuries. Since the medical work of the Greeks and the Romans had practically disappeared, the general attitude towards illness was much influenced by Christian beliefs. The acceptance of pain and disease for which there was very little relief at the time had to be sublimated by

[1] H. Chomet, *The Influence of Music on Health and Life*, pp. 211–12.
[2] H. E. Sigerist, *Civilisation and Disease*, p. 213.

some means that were spiritual or mystical, such as music, which was widely used in the Church.

In spite of the influence of the Church, certain illnesses seemed to be related to the pagan world and required the same cathartic musical treatment. The occurrence of Tarantism in certain parts of Europe puzzled many practitioners of the time. It seems to have been similar to the ancient Korybantism, a disease that provoked hysterical behaviour. Tarantism has been mentioned in a number of medical writings, all authors agreeing that the only cure for it was music and dancing. Robert Bayfield,[1] a seventeenth-century physician, describes it as 'Lascivia Chorea', arising from a malign humour and very common in Germany. The patients needed music so much that the magistrates used to hire musicians to play to them and some lusty sturdy companions to dance with. We cannot do better than to refer to Sigerist's chapter on 'disease and music', where he describes at length the history of tarantism.[2] According to him, tarantism seems to have been a kind of mental disorder occurring mainly in Apulia, but was observed as well in other European countries. It took the form of a collective dance mania affecting people of all ages and social condition.

The illness was frequently mentioned in the medical literature of the sixteenth and seventeenth centuries, but only three writers have written from their own experience, namely Epiphanius Ferdinandus, Giorgio Baglivi and Athanasius Kircher. The latter collected the text of some of the music used in the treatment of tarantism.

Apulia, an ancient Greek colony, had remained exceedingly primitive. Sigerist suggests that the dancing mania was probably a relic of old pagan rites of an orgiastic and erotic character still

[1] Robert Bayfield, Physician (1630–90), in Hunter-Macalpine, *300 Years of Psychiatry*, O.U.P. (1963), p. 170.
[2] H. E. Sigerist, *Civilisation and Disease*, pp. 216–28.

MT–D

alive in southern Italy in spite of the watchful eyes of the Church. Although it seemed to be related to pagan customs perhaps never completely rejected, the illness was attributed to the sting of the tarantula spider.

As well as being very primitive, Apulia had a well-known record or ardent fevers, frenzies, pleurisies and madness, made worse by the excessive heat of the climate and the fiery constitution of its inhabitants.

The symptoms of the illness were of a recurring type, nobody could be sure to be cured more than temporarily. The disease was worse during the hot days of summer when the tarantula was most lively. People would wake up suddenly, jump up and feel acute pain, run out of their houses, dancing madly. Many of them behaved in an obscene way, adorned themselves with garlands of vine or reeds; their behaviour was uncontrollable. The physicians who examined them could find nothing specifically wrong with them; they suffered vaguely from thirst, headaches, heart pains or fainting fits as do many neurotic people. The only effective treatment was music and dancing. It was said that people could die of the illness if music was not available at once.

Usually during the hot season bands of musicians were at hand, ready to be hired and paid for their services. Bands consisted of all kinds of instruments, many of them in the high register—violins, pipes, zithers, harps, timbrels, small drums. They played the tarantella, repeating it endlessly and very fast. The repetitive and compelling character of the music must have produced a hypnotic state and provoked hysterical behaviour, ending in a catharsis well known to the Greek.

The patients danced madly in groups, sometimes for days on end. The usual treatment was to let the patient dance himself to exhaustion from sunrise to noon. He was then put in a warm bed where he could sweat profusely. Later in the day he resumed his frantic dancing to music, followed by another sedation. The physicians thought with reason that the cure might have been caused by profuse perspiration. But when they applied the remedy by itself there was no improvement. The patient could be cured only through music and dancing.

Music suitably performed was an essential part of the treatment. We are told that if the instruments went out of tune the patients displayed such anguish and discomfort that the matter had to be remedied before they could resume their dancing.

Tarantism died out in the eighteenth century, after having provoked tremendous interest in European medical circles as a mysterious illness the cause of which could not be diagnosed. The popular belief that it was due to the sting of a spider was investigated many times and proved to be unfounded. But the fact remained that music and dancing were the only remedies for this strange illness.

It is interesting to note that the patients suffering from tarantism were not supposed to be possessed by an evil spirit. The physicians looked at them as patients requiring medical treatment.

But the new scientific outlook of the Renaissance could not completely suppress old beliefs or popular superstitions on health and illness, especially concerning mental disorder, still believed to be an evil possession. The insane were supposed to communicate with and to obey evil forces. The Church and the Law condemned them ruthlessly.

Nevertheless from the sixteenth century a very few physicians gave insanity other causes than witchcraft, which they said was contrary to reason or nature—among them Johann Weyer, Juan Luis Vives in Spain, Paracelsus the famous physician, who thought that the insane were sick people in need of humane medical or spiritual treatment.[1]

[1] H. E. Sigerist, *Civilisation and Disease*, p. 83.

The Renaissance was one of the most dynamic and creative periods of human history. The respective fields of medicine and music saw tremendous changes, because both affected man, who was discovering himself.

The new discovery of anatomy headed by Vesalius (1514–64) dominated the following centuries. It gave man a rational conception of the mechanism of his body and opened the door to modern scientific medicine based on the observation of phenomena which could be assessed in terms of causes and effects. This advance influenced all remedial means, including the use of music in medicine.

Music and all the arts had become an individual projection of man's emotional experiences and a means of communication from man to man at the human level. Moreover, man began again to enjoy beauty and harmony as a sensuous experience.

The gradual changes of attitude towards music, and towards science, are of tremendous importance to our subject. Music was becoming an important means of individual self-expression and of communication between composers, performers and listeners in which the human elements were more and more significant. The time was one of social grace in which music played a civilising influence and bound people together in the village as well as at Court. Many physicians or scientists shared the general interest in music; some of them were good amateurs and enjoyed playing or singing. The differentiation between professionals and amateurs was not marked as it is today.

A number of music-loving physicians had an inquiring mind and observed the effects of music on man, possibly on themselves, and even on animals. As the scientific link with ancient Greece had not been broken, and the great physicians of antiquity were still revered and often quoted, some physicians investigated the Greek beliefs in the therapeutic value of music. But from the seventeenth century onwards, physicians looked at the subject in terms of physiology and psychology more than from the Greek philosophical and ethical angle.

From the Renaissance onwards a surprising number of medical men have been interested in music, and not only from the medical aspect. The first History of Music which was published after his death was written by Pierre Michon Bourdelot (1610-85), physician to the King of France and Queen Christina of Sweden.[1] Many medical men of the time have written on music, health and disease, thus being the forerunners of Dr Agnes Savil[2] and Dr Sidney Licht[3] in the twentieth century.

Some physicians mention the subject more or less briefly in medical books, but others have written treatises on the effect of music on their patients and on its application in medical treatment. The physician Robert Burton was one of the first physicians of the Renaissance who observed and wrote on the healing power of music. He himself had suffered from chronic melancholy and his ideas on music might have come from his own experience.[4]

Some writers describe cases which are still of interest today. Usually the physician directed the treatment, but the music was provided by a musician as in the following case treated by Richard Brocklesby.[5] He was a London medical man, physician to the famous Dr Samuel Johnson, and wrote a complete treatise

[1] Jacques Chailley, Ibid., p. 1.
[2] Agnes Savil, M.D., Music, Health and Character, John Lane, The Bodley Head (1923).
[3] Sidney Licht, M.D., Music in Medicine, New England Conservatory of Music, Boston (1946).
[4] Robert Burton (1557-1640), The Anatomy of Melancholy, Oxford (1632).
[5] Richard Brocklesby, M.D., F.R.C.P. (1722-47), Reflections on Ancient and Modern Musick with Application to the Cure of Diseases, Cooper, London (1749).

on music therapy. The following description of one of his cases is very thorough. It shows a remarkable graduation in the techniques he used. He first describes the symptoms and causes of the illness; refers to the musical history of the patient, who was first made to listen to music again in order to provoke a motivation to play. He was provided with an audience with whom he shared a musical experience and could communicate. Relatives and friends helped towards his rehabilitation, which was complete. 'The patient was a Scottish gentleman who had lost his two sons in the defeat of Dunblain.' Brocklesby tells us that '. . . in spite of all care taken of him he fell into a nervous fever which left him in so deep a melancholy that he refused the necessary support of food and all discourse with the persons usually conversant about him: when all remedies were excluded his physician (who previously knew what delight he formerly had in playing on the harp) proposed to the patient's friends to engage one of the ablest hands on that instrument, to approach him with such soft and solemn sounds, as were formerly known to give him much delight. His relations were under no difficulty to consent to the trial, and as soon as one or two pieces had been play'd the patient discovered an uncommon emotion both of body and mind and, shortly after, reproach'd their presumption in so disturbing his meditations. When this point was once gained, the doctor enjoin'd the patient to play a while every day within audience, till by degrees the sick person was induced to speak of ordinary things; and shortly after, to take food and such medicines as were requisite in his condition, 'til at length he perfectly recovered his former state of health.'[1]

Many physicians who probably enjoyed music themselves as a recreation and a way to refresh their minds recognised the value of music as a comfort, a diversion from obsession or 'dreade and besy thoughts'. The physician Philip Barrough said of his mental

[1] Richard Brocklesby, ibid., pp. 34, 35.

patients, 'Let them be merry as much as may be and have musical instruments and singing.'[1]

Ambroise Paré advised his surgical patients to have a consort of violins and violons to make them merry.[2]

Richard Browne, a forerunner of Brocklesby, had been more explicit when he stated in an essay on music and illness that 'In nervous disorders such as hypocondriack, hysterick and melancholicks affection, singing will be much conducive of the cure: for as these diseases of the mind filled with gloomy dejecting ideas and the body labours under a deficiency of spirits, and as by singing we may possibly strive the Ear so pleasingly as to affect the mind and divert one's anxious thoughts by the succession of brisk and lively ideas of the tune; we may certainly by this means chear and elevate the soul and by sympathy invigorate the motions of the spirits.'[3]

Little by little the authors took a more scientific approach. Some of them became aware that music could act on the body as well as on the mind. Already in the eighteenth century we find a certain amount of research on the purely physiological effect of music. This followed rationally the growing medical knowledge in physiology and neurology. The writers discovered some relation between bodily and musical rhythm, pulse and musical beat. They observed the effect of music on breathing, blood pressure or digestion. Richard Browne[4] thought that singing 'influences the motion of the heart, the circulation of the blood, the digestion, the lungs and breathing. In singing the pressure of the air upon the lungs is greater than in common expiration.' He studied its application in cases of respiratory disorder. He

[1] Philip Barrough (1560–1590), *300 Years of Psychiatry*, Hunter and Macalpine, O.U.P., pp. 24–28.

[2] D. W. Singer, *Ambroise Paré*, p. 234.

[3] Richard Browne (Apothecary in Oakham, Rutland): *Medicina Musica*, John Crooke, Printer, Nottingham (1729), pp. 28–29.

[4] Richard Browne, ibid., p. 12.

found that singing would be injurious in case of pleurisy, pneumonia or any inflammatory disorder of the lungs, because of the immediate action upon that organ. But in periodical chronic asthma he believed that if the patient exercised his lungs by singing in the intervals between the attacks it might prevent a return of or alleviate the paroxysm.[1]

Louis Roger,[2] a French physician, wrote a serious book on the effects of music on the human body in which he was more critical, emphasised the need for scientific observation and experiments, and he discarded much of the irrational work done in the past.

In the nineteenth century a growing concern in the medical treatment of mental and physical illness gave physicians an interest in ancillary therapeutic means. Dr Hector Chomet[3] in 1846 wrote a treatise on 'The Influence of Music on Health and Life' based on a paper he read before the Paris Academy of Sciences—a fact which shows the interest of a learned body in the subject. The work is comprehensive, it contains much data and discusses the use of music as a help in the prevention and treatment of illness. Some of his conclusions are still valid today.

J. E. D. Esquirol (1772–1840), the renowned psychiatrist, recommended music, but he was more guarded about its effects. The following extract from his book *Insanity in Mental Maladies* shows that he knew very little about music and must have used it without discrimination. He did not try to relate the reactions of his patients to the type of music used or to the manner in which it was offered. Perhaps he would have been more successful

[1] Richard Brown, ibid., p. 26.
[2] *Traité des Effets de la Musique sur le Corps Humain*, Paris (*1748*). 'The Renaissance and 17th and 18th Centuries', Armen Carapetyan, in *Music and Medicine*, ed. Schoen and Schullivan, pp. 146–7.
[3] Hector Chomet, *The Influence of Music on Health and Life*.

in following Pargeter's advice, although he gave the matter his serious consideration. He wrote: 'I have often employed music but have rarely been successful with it. It brings peace and composure of mind, but does not cure. I have seen those whom music rendered furious: one because all the tones appeared false; another because he thought it dreadful that others should amuse themselves near a wretch like him. . . . However it is a valuable remedial agent, particularly in convalescence. It ought not to be neglected, however indeterminate may be the principles of application, or uncertain its efficacy.'[1]

We propose to discuss in a later chapter the observation that 'all the tones appeared false' to one of the patients; indeed, all the reactions he describes are worth examining.

If the opinions of many of these writers are debatable or even unacceptable today, they are serious and within the medical knowledge of the day. Perhaps Brocklesby's approach was the nearest to ours when he saw music as a help to medical treatment: 'Now if it were found practical in some cases to soothe the turbulent affections, and appease the disorderly springs of fancy, as it were to re-establish the former union of the body and mind by the powers of music, in that interval of time, proper medicines might be administered to better purpose . . .'[2]

At the end of the eighteenth century Pargeter (1760–1810) was one of the first physicians to understand that a specific musical knowledge was necessary to control its therapeutic uses. We may be surprised that his sensible advice is not more widely followed today. The following lines are significant of his attitude and we may notice that he calls music a science: 'If those who have the direction of music in maniacal disorders happen to understand the *theory* of that *science* there will be a greater

[1] Quoted by Hunter and Macalpine, *300 Years of Psychiatry*, p. 377.
[2] Richard Brocklesby. Quoted by Hunter and Macalpine, *300 Years of Psychiatry*, p. 378.

possibility of success than if it is introduced injudiciously. . . . A considerable share of knowledge in music, then, will be requisite to select these compositions and instruments, and the arrangements of instrumental parts, as may with an exact correspondence with the *pathos animi* attract and fascinate the attention, and influence the temper of animal spirits.'[1]

Nevertheless Chomet and others still believed that the physician himself could apply music if he possessed the necessary knowledge, as stated in the following passage: 'If we would apply music to the treatment or relief of disease we must necessarily be acquainted with the patient's manner of life, his character, temperament, habits and passions. The physician, being enlightened in all these peculiarities, will select the most suitable airs, being careful as regards rhythms, set them in fittings keys and adapt them to the proper instruments. . . . The choice of musical compositions, the proper moment for applying them, a correct appreciation of the patient's constitution, comprise the whole secret of this method of cure . . . the success of this *musical treatment* will be all the more marked, if directed by a skilful hand.'[2]

Another medical man, Benoit Mojan, in the nineteenth century suggested some principles of application, but does not mention who should be in charge of the music. 'When the doctor wants to prescribe music in the treatment of illness he must take into consideration: (1) the nature of the illness; (2) the taste of the patient for certain tunes or others; (3) the effect that may be produced on him by certain melodies preferably to others; (4) the use of music is to be avoided in cases of headaches, earaches and in all cases where there is excessive excitability in the system; (5) the physician must be careful to moderate the sounds, since their intensity could stimulate too strongly; (6) the sounds

[1] Quoted by Hunter and Macalpine; *300 Years of Psychiatry*, p. 376.
[2] Hector Chomet, *The Influence of Music on Health and Life*, p. 233.

should increase gradually, be varied and the music should not last for long.'[1]

We may notice that Mojan advocates the assessment of the patient's musical sensitivity, the control of volume of sounds, and recommends short performances, according to the reduced span of attention of any patient.

A premature but interesting experiment in music therapy was undertaken in London at the end of the nineteenth century, some details of which were published in The Lancet (July and August 1891) and in the British Medical Journal (19 and 26 September 1891). The promoter was Canon F. K. Harford, not a medical man but a proficient musician, and his scheme had only a brief life. It consisted of forming a small choir of ladies, accompanied by a harp and muted violins, who would perform in a room adjoining the patients'. He recommended that the ladies should be anonymous, unseen by the patients and paid for their services.

Canon Harford also saw the necessity of collecting data and gaining the physicians' support. His ideas met with some interest in the medical world, as well as with much criticism or irrational enthusiasm. The plan petered out, but some of his ideas are still valid today and put into practice.[2]

This may be the only early instance of a therapeutic plan devised by a musician and not by a medical man. In the course of history until the twentieth century the music was applied by the physician who prescribed it unless he called in musicians who were not trained in therapeutic methods. The personal relationship between the musician and the patient which Canon

[1] Benoit Mojan, Dr in Medicine and Surgery, 'Sur l'Utilité de la Musique' (1803), translated from the Italian into French, Pub. Fournier, Rome, New York Public Libraries.

[2] Dr E. Ashworth Underwood, 'Apollo and Terpsichore', Bulletin of the History of Medicine, Vol. XXI, No. 5, September-October 1947, pp. 669.

Harford discarded was nevertheless of the same great importance as today and played an important part in the success or the failure of the treatment.

11. THE MUSIC THERAPIST

Until the twentieth century the part musicians played in music therapy was empirical. They were not meant to understand the therapeutic effect of music in which the physician was interested. The names of two musicians stand out in the history of music therapy, namely David the harp player and Farinelli the singer. The two stories have been told with many details, but references to the musicians have often omitted significant facts.

We find in the two stories the essential factors involved in music therapy, namely: the personality and the illness of the patient; the personality and the musical skill of the musician; their interpersonal relationship; the varying effects of the music according to the actual mood of the patient. But these factors have never been fully analysed in terms of music therapy.

David and Saul

In the ancient history of Israel we find several texts on the effect of music on the prophets. The harp player was instrumental in provoking a mystical pathological state during which they prophesied. 'Now bring me a minstrel,' said Elisha. 'And it came to pass, when the minstrel played, that the hand of the Lord came upon him'[1] and he prophesied.

In the story of David and Saul, music was used to relieve a neurotic depression. Thus David was one of the first musicians to be called in and to use his musical skill with a mentally affected person.

Only a short passage in the story[2] has been selected and used

[1] 2 Kings iii. 15.
[2] 1 Kings xvi.23.

ad nauseam by physicians, therapists and others, but they have stopped there and not discussed the psychological changes that altered the relationship between the two individuals and ultimately destroyed the effects of the music.

From the beginning the two personalities are well described and in full contrast: Saul was of very humble origin. He came from the least of the families of the smallest tribe of Israel.[1] When he became King he developed a kind of megalomania of a paranoid type. He did not keep God's commands[2] and Samuel accused him of rebellion and stubbornness.[3] We are even told that 'The Lord repented that He had made Saul King over Israel'.[4]

Saul exhibited symptoms of mental disorder. He suffered from recurring fits of melancholia during which God's spirit departed from him, and from uncontrollable fits of anger. He had received the gift of prophecy, which we often find associated with mental disorder. This might have been epilepsy, the 'sacred disease' of the Greeks.

In contrast, David was a pure and holy young man. He is described as a comely person, ruddy and 'of a beautiful countenance, goodly to look to'.[5] He developed into a mighty valiant man of war and was 'prudent in matters', and the Lord was with him.[6] We know that he could love deeply, that he was incapable of hatred, rebellion or injustice. Moreover, he was an excellent musician, a cunning player on the harp.[7] After having become King, he celebrated his victories in playing before the Lord on 'all manners of instruments made of fine wood, even on harps and psalteries, and on timbrels, and on cornets and on cymbals'.[8]

In the first part of the story Saul's recurring fits of depression were of great concern to his attendants, who tried to find a remedy for his melancholia. They begged him 'to seek out a man

[1] Ibid., ix.21.   [2] Ibid., xiii.13.   [3] Ibid., xv.23.   [4] Ibid., xv.35.
[5] 1 Kings xvi.12.   [6] Ibid., xvi.18.   [7] Ibid., xvi.18.   [8] 2 Kings vi.5.

who is a cunning player on an harp: and it shall come to pass, when the evil spirit from God is upon thee, that he shall play with his hand and thou shalt be well'.[1] This advice shows a current belief in the power of music over the spirit. And thus David was brought before the King.

David found immediate favour in Saul's sight, who appointed him his armour-bearer. David loved Saul greatly and respected him. When the evil spirit was upon Saul, he played and the King was refreshed and was well. The music had a therapeutic effect, probably increased by the pleasure Saul had in the presence of a loving and attractive boy, who seems to have possessed a quiet and stable personality. We are not told about the music he played on the harp, but we gather that it was instrumental and not vocal.

In the second part of the story Saul's feelings for David underwent a drastic change. David's return after his successes in the war against the Philistines, and the glowing praise he received from the women, provoked in the King insane jealousy possibly inflamed by the homosexual character of his relationship. We are told that 'he eyed David from that day and forward',[2] perhaps concealing his animosity. 'He became David's enemy continually.'[3] Moreover, Saul was more and more afraid of David and of his wisdom,[4] because the Lord was with him. Fear was bound to increase his hatred. Under these circumstances no means used by David to comfort Saul could have succeeded.

One morning the evil spirit from God came again upon Saul. On that day he seemed to have been worse than ever, showing signs of extreme disturbance such as prophesying in the middle of the house. David played to the King as usual, on his harp. But Saul, who was harbouring against him hidden and murderous thoughts which he could not control, cast his javelin at the player

[1] I Kings xvi.16.　　[2] I Kings xviii.9.　　[3] Ibid., viii.29.
[4] Ibid., xviii.12, 15, 29.

and tried to smite him. David escaped, but had to fly for his life.[1]

Although this occurred several times, David showed towards Saul continuous feelings of love and respect and refused to take revenge on him when the occasion presented itself.[2] In the end Saul, humbling himself, acknowledged David as a better and more righteous man.[3] After the violent episodes following David's playing on the harp, there is no more mention of Saul's fits of melancholia, or of David playing on the harp.

Farinelli and the Spanish King

In the stories of David and of Farinelli the two patients suffered from a similar kind of mental disorder, but the personalities of the musicians and of the patients were different in every respect, and so was their relationship. The success of Farinelli's treatment was due to his musical style and achievement, even before the King had set eyes on him. Farinelli did not play an instrument 'with his hand'. His art was entirely vocal.

When the King first heard him the singer was out of sight in an adjoining room. It was the impact of his music alone that shook the patient out of his state of despondency and was responsible for his first reaction. From the first day to the last the relationship between King and singer was peaceful, harmonious and affectionate.

We find in *Grove's Dictionary of Music* the history of Farinelli's amazing musical career, and many details from which conclusions may be drawn. Farinelli, born in 1705, was the greatest Italian castrato singer of his time, and an exceptional personality. He was famous through his triumphs in opera, loaded with honours and wealth. His style was then one fitting to the stage of the day, of extraordinary brilliance and bravura expected by the fashionable audiences. In 1731 Farinelli visited Vienna and for some unknown reason studied new methods which deeply

[1] Ibid., xix.9, 10.   [2] 1 Kings xxiv.4, 5.   [3] Ibid., xxiv.17.

modified his style. From one of mere glamour and virtuosity he transformed it into a style of simplicity, sincerity and pathos. This probably gave his singing a quality of expression and intimacy which was deeper but not so fashionable as his former style.

We may presume that either the singer had gone through some emotional experience which transformed his attitude towards music, or he was a great artist always seeking for achievement greater than brilliance and fame. It was said at the time that 'the successes he obtained in his youth did not prevent him from continuing to study; and this great artist applied himself with such perseverance that he contrived to change his style and to acquire another and superior method when his name was already famous and his fortune brilliant'.[1] Such a development might have explained his subsequent success at the Spanish Court, and the renouncement of his operatic career which followed.

In 1737, in the midst of triumphal European tours, Farinelli went to Spain on a short visit. He arrived in Madrid at the time Philip V was suffering from acute melancholia. The King had for many weeks refused to take part in the affairs of state, and this put the whole country in a critical situation. The Queen had the idea of inviting Farinelli to sing in a room adjoining that where the King was sitting, dejected, unshaven, unkempt and withdrawn. Hoping that appealing music might reach the King and bring him out of his depression, she asked Farinelli to choose some expressive and pathetic melodies—the kind of music that fitted both the singer's new style and the patient's melancholic state. The King heard the music from his room and was so moved by the unexpected experience that he came out of his lethargic state, sent for the singer to thank him and asked him to choose

[1] G. Mancini, quoted in *Grove's Dictionary of Music and Musicians*, Vol. II, p. 200.

his reward for this beautiful music. Farinelli, whose mission seemed to have been successful, asked the King to return to his normal life and to fulfil his royal duties. The monarch agreed, was shaved for the first time in many weeks, left his room and returned to the affairs of state. From then he performed all the functions attributed to him, including the vital one of presiding over the Council of State.

Music had made the King come out of his depressive state when everything else had failed to move him. Farinelli's story does not end here. He was immediately engaged as personal singer to the King and for this he renounced his brilliant career as a virtuoso, a sacrifice that no money or Court honours could repay. He said that during ten years until the death of Philip V he sang the same four songs to the King every night without change of any kind. Two of those were 'Pallido il sole' and 'Per questo dolce amplesso' of Hasse. The third was a minuet on which he improvised variations. Thus in the course of ten years he repeated about 3,600 times the same pieces, and never sang anything else to the King. We may suppose that the pieces had been so successful that the King asked for them every day.

Hasse was a contemporary popular composer. His melodies are not published. We know that they were pleasing, without depth, but musically and vocally attractive. The improvised variations on the minuet must have brought in some changes, but on the same theme. We do not know Farinelli's opinion of this repetitive process. As a performing musician he probably might have preferred a change out of his vast repertoire of songs. As a therapist he must have thought that the best was what succeeded.

The King, who led a normal life until his death, must have found relaxation in familiar pieces that brought a feeling of security. Other pieces might have disturbed or excited him at a time when he wanted to relax and sleep. The melodies were softly expressive and the rhythm of a minuet is not physically stimulating.

The relationship between the two men had begun objectively without any of the first personal contact that had made David agreeable to Saul. In this sense alone it was real music therapy through the effect of music. This lack of emotional strain explains why Philip V and the castrato's relationship remained one of devoted service, gratitude and affection. Farinelli until the King's death enjoyed his friendship and confidence. Although he became the first favourite of his successor, Ferdinand VI, who loved music, and even acquired a certain political influence, he mourned Philip V and his Queen until the end of his life.[1]

The musicians of the two stories were skilled performers and had the ability to communicate through their art. Throughout history the healer-musician has possessed the skill and knowledge necessary to use the musical means available at the time.

The magician is known to have possessed a vast repertoire of specific songs for certain kinds of illness which he trusted jealously to his memory. He also used drums, rattles, bells and flutes according to a ritual related to the type of illness. At a later stage the Greek physician possessed much musical knowledge and was able to understand and even analyse music as an art and a science.

In more modern times some physicians experimenting with music displayed a certain musical knowledge, not always as performers, and not always adequate, and which would not be sufficient for today's requirements.

We are in an age of specialisation. Much medical work is done today by a team whose members understand one another and work towards a common aim. But their contact with the patient is often diminished. Before this age a patient could more easily relate personally to the physician. This is not the case today,

[1] From *Grove's Dictionary of Music and Musicians*, Vol. II, pp. 198–200.

except with the general physician, who is usually not responsible for the specialised treatment. Specialisation increases the gap between the patient and the doctor, as between knowledge and ignorance.

There would be danger of even increasing the remoteness of the specialist if there was not another trend in medicine, which gives a special place to various therapies. We are more and more conscious of the psychological factors involved in any kind of illness; mental health comes increasingly into the total picture. The fact that physicians definitely recognise the value of ancillary therapies in medical treatment is proof that they see the patient as a many-sided individual to be approached from different angles.

The therapist can bring to the treatment a human relationship of a personal and even intimate character. He is not as remote as the consultant and more approachable as a person. The ancillary therapists as well as the nurses play an important psychological part in the recovery of the patient, irrespective of their professional skill.

Whatever his personality, age or sex, the modern music therapist is first and foremost a musician and should be considered as such. The physiotherapist works on his physiological knowledge, the music therapist works on his understanding of music and its effects on mind, body and emotions. He should also be familiar with the phenomenon of transference which occurs sometimes when the patient projects on the therapist some of his unsolved problems. The situation should be handled on psychiatric lines at its early stages, since the patient may become too dependent on the music therapist. Moreover in an analytical situation the relationship should not involve a third person.

Music is a many-sided art, which includes craft as well as musicianship, and is based on the perception and interpretation of sound and of its symbols. Music therapy works, as it has done

throughout the ages, on the various effects of sound even before
it has become organised in music. These effects are multifarious;
they react on one another, and require a special study and discussion, if we wish to understand the application of music
therapy.

12. THE ELEMENTS OF MUSIC

Even in its most simple forms, music is evocative of sensations,
moods and emotions. It can reflect the feeling of the moment or
change it by its presence. It can also increase the actual mood
and bring it to a climax, or dispel it. The lonely piper in the
woods, the invisible drummer on the hills, create a mood by
their actions, and so does the symphonic orchestra performing
in a large auditorium. The music-makers are themselves affected
by their own playing.

Music has the power to affect mood because it contains suggestive, persuasive or even compelling elements. In music
accompanying a specific function one of these elements is usually
dominant. But whatever its purpose music is always related to
man's own experiences, since it has been born out of his mind,
speaks of his emotions, and lies within his perceptual range. It
has the power to reach him. It has been said that music penetrates into the most secret recesses of the soul, an effect against
which man is more or less defenceless.

The therapeutic effects of music have been observed throughout history, sometimes very accurately. But there are far fewer
references to the kind of music that was used. This lack creates
a void in the knowledge we could gain from past experiments,
and we have to rely on our present observations. We can vaguely
deduce from old texts the kind of music which created certain
feelings and provoked a certain behaviour. But these observations are too general to lead to a controlled application of music.

Even today too many of the observations relate to a general
effect made by pieces of music played from beginning to end, or

they speak of a general reaction to the music of a composer, for instance to Brahms or to Schumann, irrespective of the character of a specific piece. Progress in constructive therapeutic work should rest on the patient's response to certain musical elements, from which we can formulate and apply our principles. The elements that we propose to discuss combine together in different ways to make a finished product in which there is usually a dominant factor. Responses to a musical experience may be as complex as the combination of the elements present in the music. In assessing therapeutically the patient's reactions, we may have to consider them in the light of each of these elements before coming to a conclusion.

The character of music and the effects it provokes depend on the different elements of sound and their relationship. These are as follows:

(1) frequency (or musical pitch)
(2) intensity
(3) tone colour
(4) interval, creating melody and harmony
(5) duration, creating rhythm and tempo.

Some elements, pitch, intensity and tone colour are inherent parts of sound as an acoustical substance, and even animals can react to them. They provoke what Altshuler calls 'thalamic responses'[1] to sensations which need not be interpreted by the higher functions of the brain. They do not carry a symbolic or intellectual meaning. Nevertheless each of them is a vital factor in the emotional power of music.

The other elements which give music a form and an expressive meaning are those produced by a relationship between sounds, usually rhythm, melody and harmony. Their apprehension requires some intellectual process, however low.

[1] Ira M. Altshuler, *Retrospect and Perspective*, M.T. (1952) The Allen Press, Lawrence, Kansas, p. 15.

Pitch. Frequency or pitch in musical terms is produced by the number of vibrations of a sound. It usually acts on man at a purely physical level and in a rational way. On the whole, very rapid vibrations are a strong nervous stimulus, slow ones have a relaxing effect. Nervous or tense people may be badly affected by high frequency, especially if it lasts too long, although in music its effects can be mitigated by the presence of other elements of a relaxing kind, such as softness or tone colour. This can be observed in the muting of a very high note which corrects the effect of tension.

Intensity. The intensity of a sound depends on the amplitude of the vibrations, which affects its volume and its carrying power. The intensity of a musical sound goes from the nearly inaudible to the deafening. It plays a great part in the effect of music and may be almost in itself a means of gratification. If an unsophisticated listener prefers symphonic to chamber music it may be due to its large volume irrespective of the interest or the musical value of the composition.

We may here quote a curious remark made at the beginning of this century, long before our era of noise in every field. Herman Smith observed that among the strange characteristics of man was his manifest taste for exaggerated noises.[1]

It is true that a continuous large volume of music makes on some listeners a satisfying effect of plenitude, and may even give them a feeling of protection against physical or psychological intrusion. This can be observed in music of very different styles, such as Bach's choral music or Tchaikovsky's symphonies, which may produce a similar effect on an unsophisticated listener. The youth who carries with him a loud-playing transistor is often an insecure being in need of some protection against the surrounding world. The full tone of an organ filling a church

[1] Herman Smith, *The World's Earliest Music Traced in its Beginning in Ancient Lands,* London (1900), Ch. XIX.

is a protection against the vastness or loftiness of the building.

If music is loud enough, it can also help to obliterate unwanted sounds. Long before the emergence of mechanised background music, we are told that in the Greek temples and during certain ceremonies music helped to suppress unexpected sounds that would have been of bad omen.

Intensity is a dynamic element that can be manipulated. It moves in time through many shades of growing and diminishing strength, creates within the sound various relationships of loudness and softness, climaxes and anticlimaxes. These may give an impression of some power approaching or receding and even evoke a primeval fear of sound.

In reverse, soft volume may produce a feeling of intimacy, speak to the timid or the withdrawn, persuade instead of coercing or intruding. It reflects quietness or serenity which may irritate a listener in need of strong sensations. At the same time softness when accompanied by rhythm can give an impression of strength.

As such, all degrees of volume or intensity provoke simple emotions. Playing loud or soft is the first means of expression to be used by a beginner in music, when an emotion provokes a physical impulse in the performer.

Tone Colour. Tone colour or timbre which depends on the harmonies present in any particular sound is one of the most suggestive elements in music. Our vocabulary is so restricted that we have to use the word 'colour' to qualify one of the most important elements contained in a musical sound and which has a deep psychological significance because of its associative power.

Tone colour is a non-rhythmical, purely sensuous element that produces in the listener a pleasurable non-intellectual impression against which he does not erect a defence mechanism. We can observe this in the effect made by certain pieces by Chopin or Debussy, by the lower notes of the flute or the sound of the celesta. The sensuous effect of tone colour in itself has sometimes been considered as beneficial or harmful, usually on ethical grounds. For instance, we are told by Aristotle[1] that in Athens at some time a few antique instruments such as the dulcimers or psalteries were rejected because they seemed merely to tickle the ears of the audience.

In primitive society, and because of its imitative character, the timbre of the tone expressed an individuality and was associated with the magic Iso principle. The human voice or the musical instruments were made to imitate a particular sound in order to propitiate, or to have power over, the dead or alive owner of the sound. Many of these natural sounds became musically organised patterns, but kept their tone colour, as we can hear in the speaking drums of Africa. Even today many primitive musical instruments imitate the sound of the rain or the wind even when they have lost their magical power. This applies to the human voice, and to the impression made by its tone colour. Schneider has observed that the timbre and compass of a singing voice alone or an instrument may induce a certain feeling of comfort or disquiet. Primitive erotic or funeral music are sung in a peculiar nasal voice, and it is often the type of voice that determines the character of the melody.[2]

We can notice today that the physical effect produced by the peculiar tone of certain jazz wind instruments creates a definite climate without which the rhythmical elements would not be so effective.

The effect of tone colour goes very deep. Darwin might have suggested that it had biological roots. An infant left free to choose spontaneously between sound-making objects easy to manipulate often shows a marked preference for one of them; he

[1] Aristotle, *Politics*, Book V, Ch. VI, p. 243.
[2] Marius Schneider, 'Primitive Music', *New Oxford History of Music*, Vol. I, pp. 1–60.

returns again and again to the same one whose sound makes a particular appeal to him.

There is in tone colour even today a mysterious power. The same piece played or sung by two performers of the same standard may have a markedly different effect on the listener because of the personal quality of the performer's vocal or instrumental tone. The musical importance of this personal quality is paramount because it creates an immediate communication between the interpreter and the listener at a non-intellectual or non-critical level. The sensuous quality of a beautiful tone needs no mental effort or musical education to be enjoyed. In many compositions the blending of the tone of different instruments produces a colourful effect which appeals even to an unsophisticated listener. In 'La Mer' or 'Le Clair de Lune' the listener is literally bathing in the atmosphere surrounding him.

Interval. Interval, based on the distance between two notes, is closely related to pitch. It consists of the relationship between two musical sounds of a series and results in melody and harmony.

Man has organised sounds in musical symbols which vary according to his culture. Therefore certain music can reach only the man who belongs to that culture or has been educated in the understanding of its meaning.

We have seen that each of the Greek scales was supposed to create a specific mood solely because of the intervals which it contained. Today we are using the ancient pentatonic scale of five notes when music absolutely free of tension is required. It contains no intervals which would create a problem and need a solution.

The combination of sounds into series of intervals can be pleasant or unpleasant to the ear. According to the laws of harmony in our Western music certain notes are attracted or repelled by one another, or even stay indifferent, according to the scale of sounds they belong to. Therefore these combinations are endowed with a temporal life made of movement and conflicts and solutions related to the feelings they express. Before coming to a harmonious conclusion a musical composition may contain, as life does, many dissonances which are to the individual either stimulating or irritating or disturbing. He may even relate to some tense or dissonant interval which reflects his inner state. But whatever happens in the course of the musical development, there is, at the end, a solution.

A harmonic progression has a meaning, it holds the attention in time until the final conclusion. The feeling given by a musical sequence, however dissonant, ending in a harmonious orderly way, brings emotional satisfaction to the listener and the performer alike.

Rhythm. Rhythm is the most dynamic, therefore the most conspicuous element in music. It is combined with pitch and tone colour and gives them final significance. It expresses an alternation of tension and relaxation through stresses, accentuations, breathing spaces, strong and weak beats.

The duration of each of the musical sounds is stated explicitly on the musical notation, and rhythm is related to their relationship. But a phrase played in mechanical strict time according to the duration of each note has very little meaning. Rhythm is not measurable in terms of exact timing, because it carries with it a human emotion of stress and repose.

The various effects of rhythm are easy to observe and extremely diverse, sometimes even opposite. Rhythm can provoke hysterical behaviour or induce sleep. It may create an awareness of movement or have an hypnotic effect.

Rhythm is not necessarily the percussive element commonly evoked by the word. Unobtrusive soft rhythm exists in music and can be very much alive. Such rhythm may give an impression of peaceful security because it occurs at regular intervals as expected and sometimes is felt unconsciously as in the rhythm of certain physical functions. A melody, however calm, possesses an inner rhythm similar to the rhythm of a line in drawing. 'The Swan' by Saint-Saëns is of that order, as well as numerous lullabies or melodies carrying tender and orderly feelings regulated by a simple repetitive rhythm.

A repetitive or obsessive rhythm can be psychologically depressing when it seems to express a neurotic condition. A pertinent remark was made by a depressed patient on one of Chopin's Nocturnes. She found it depressing because of the obstinate repeated note in the bass. She thought that it sounded as if he could not get rid of this note and there was no solution to be found.

The perception of a repeated continuous sound at a slow pace and getting slower and slower may obliterate consciousness, especially if the melody accompanying the rhythm is of a non-ending type and suppresses the sense of time.

On the other hand, rhythm is symbolically related to will-power and self-control. As such, it is orderly, physically strong and makes an invigorating effect on the listener and performer alike. Such rhythm is the most vital element in the music of certain composers, such as Beethoven or Dvorak.

In England during the last war the initial pattern of the Fifth Symphony became the symbol of the will to resist tyranny. Even dissociated from its text it is in itself an energetic rhythmical pattern which brought hope and strength to oppressed people throughout Europe.

Rhythm can also be impulsive, and express sudden unexpected feelings. The surprise of a stress on a beat expected to be weak; the absence of a conventional accentuation; the lack of breathing spaces, all these can bring a feeling of disquiet unless it is part of an accepted style familiar to the listener or the performer.

Some primitive rhythms have developed into a nest of complexity which our Western music has not yet assimilated. But we have become more and more aware of the power of primitive music and art to stir up in us primitive feelings. We adopted the American negro jazz at the beginning of this century. Certain modern Western composers as early as Ravel and Stravinsky have been the first ones to integrate primitive rhythms in extremely sophisticated music. This is the reason why some of their music can appeal to the unsophisticated listener in spite of the refinement of the harmony and the complexity of the form.

Musical form is the regulating element in music; it follows an intellectual order and keeps the emotions it provokes within boundaries of time. When rhythmical music repeats itself endlessly without the restraint of form, there is no limit to its effects on primitive instincts. Very often jazz or other kindred music does not provide a safety valve for the listener, and it is not meant to sublimate emotions or passions as other kinds of music do. The frenzy of tribal or witches' dances, of bacchic orgies, was produced by music made of endless repetitive and conflicting rhythms at a pace faster than the heart beat, and often at an accelerating speed. Jacques Chailley is of the opinion that when such rhythmical music reaches the primitive instincts of man and unbridles them its effect may be a destructive and uncontrollable behaviour. This happened many times in musical history. He thinks that in our modern society the nostalgia for 'active' music such as the primitive has never been so alive. It is not by chance that the twentieth century began on the savage incantations of the 'Rite of Spring'.[1]

Music based on primitive rhythm and on suggestive tone colour makes on the young generation an effect which amounts to a social, more than a musical, phenomenon, and seems to be almost universal. Chailley describes such an occurrence in Paris in the early fifties: On an evening in October 1955 the manager of the Olympia Music Hall in Paris called for the help of the

[1] Jacques Chailley, *40,000 Years of Music*, p. 57.

police. Excited by the saxophone of a famous jazz band, the audience of young people below twenty years old had become hysterical, breaking windows and destroying the seats in the hall. There were many wounded and enormous damage. . . . For one hour music was as it was in primitive times, a fearful power whose secret the gods had revealed . . . which enabled man to transform the mind of others and even to give orders to the gods.[1]

Beat music has now replaced jazz in the popular favour of young undiscriminating audiences. It seems to answer the nostalgia for primitive experiences. The beat generation, says David McReynolds, is the 'expression of a generation international in character and deeply rooted in the chaos of our society which is only rational but *no longer sane*, a society which because it has divorced man from its intuitive self, can talk calmly of waging nuclear war'.[2]

The following opinion may explain the extreme musical poverty of beat music, as well as its appeal to the young of a certain type:

'The beat generation's worship of primitivism and spontaneity is more than a cover for hostility to intelligence, it arises from a pathetic poverty of feeling as well.'[3]

This is not the place to comment on the immaturity of this music and its words. We are not concerned with the aesthetic value of beat or similar music but with its effects. It seems to answer the need for sexually immature emotions of a certain age group who crowd together in the unrepressed worship of a hero and become hysterical in the process. This phenomenon can be observed in all kinds of societies today, even behind the Iron

[1] Jacques Chailley, ibid., p. 53.
[2] David McReynolds, in *The Beats*, ed. by Seymour Krim. Fawcett Publications Ltd, Gold Medal Books, U.S.A. (1960, 2nd ed. 1963), p. 1.
[3] Norman Podhoretz, ibid., p. 122.

Curtain. We have read in *The Times* of 28 July 1964 that in Prague ten youths were condemned to sentences from four to ten months for whistling, stamping their feet and wrecking furniture during a big-beat concert. We are far from the harmless rattles advocated by Aristotle for destructive youngsters.

PART TWO

THE MODERN APPLICATION
OF MUSIC
IN MEDICAL TREATMENT

1 & 2 MAGICAL HEALING WITH MUSIC
African primitive rites, Belgian Congo, Pool region

3   DAVID AND SAUL, by Carle Van Loo, engraved by Cochin

III

Physiological and Psychological Effects of Music

THROUGHOUT history man has observed with curiosity and interest the effects of music on himself and others. He has speculated and wondered at certain phenomena which were occurring again and again under the influence of music. On the whole, music has made on man the effects he expected from its use, either integrated with various functions or as a purely aesthetic experience.

It is always difficult to dissociate the physiological and the psychological effects of music. Throughout the centuries among philosophers, physicians and musicians there have been various schools of thought which have tried to explain the mechanism of the responses to music. They oscillated between two theories: some of them believed that music primarily affected the emotions and created moods which in turn acted on the body; others thought that the process worked in reverse, from the physiological to the psychological.

The contemporary philosopher Suzan Langer thinks that nervous excitement creates emotion, an opinion generally shared today. She states that 'Naturalistically inclined critics often mediate the comparison between the forms of music and those of feelings by assuming that music exhibits patterns of excitation occurring in the nervous tissues which are the physical sources of emotion.'[1] A child music therapist, Louise E. Weir, has

[1] Suzan Langer, *Philosophy in a New Key*, Harvard University Press (1951), p. 227.

MT—F

expressed the same thought 'that sound affects the autonomous nervous system which is the basis of our emotional reaction'.[1]

Most of the time the two processes react on one another. We can dissociate them only through a careful analysis. The following case is quite typical, of the old neurotic widow who said that she disliked the sound of the trumpet because it hurt her ears. This might have been a genuine nervous reaction. But it was found out that her husband, with whom she had had very bad relations, played the trumpet and that she had violently objected to it. Her disagreeable response to the sound of the instrument could have been caused either by its brassy tone or by the painful associations it brought to her memory.

Throughout history man's responses to music have been basically similar and influenced by the same factors, namely man's physical receptivity to sound, his innate or acquired sensitiveness to music, and his state of mind at the time. Conditioning due to prejudices, environment, education and other non-musical factors play an important part in these responses. We cannot ignore them.

Man can respond only to music of his culture, which conveys to him some meaning and emotion. His culture is not only ethnographical, since even in the same society people's responses to artistic experiences vary according to their social or educational background. In the same society we may find people who have been deprived of certain musical contacts—or have had music forced on them; others have discovered music by themselves without any guidance. Some ignore or accept only a certain kind of music, out of personal or social prejudices. Good listeners may be trained or born, they are not necessarily discriminating. These factors are among the many which may help

[1] Louise E. Weir, *MT* (*Music Therapy*), Proceedings of the National Association for Music Therapy, Lawrence, Kansas, The Allen Press (1952), pp. 129–32.

or hinder the work of the music therapist who tries to offer his patients an enjoyable and effective means of communication.

In therapy the best music *of its kind* is likely to be more effective, since any function is best fulfilled by the best suitable means. The best here is what succeeds, not according to an orthodox assessment of 'good' or 'bad' music, but to the response it can elicit from the patient. Whatever its kind or its aesthetic value, all music possesses the same elements we have described in the last chapter.

Apart from a few exceptions due to a mental or nervous state, patients usually react normally to the elements of music, to their dynamism, to their sensory, emotional and intellectual appeal. They react normally to the conventional character of so-called 'gay', 'sad', exciting or soothing music. In most cases we may assess their reactions on a norm common to all people. But some exceptions can be found, for instance in some cases of athetosis or schizophrenia, to be discussed later. Also we may notice some unexpected incongruous emotional reactions not at all due to the illness but to the association of the music with past memories: for instance, when a gay, light-hearted tune reminds the patient of a distressing event in his past life.

It may also happen that a patient with a good musical history now rejects anything that seems to invade the privacy of his inner life, a 'precious secret life' for some of them. We have met the rejection of music in some psychotic or autistic patients who refuse or even fight against human contacts. These may even cover their ears or their face when the music starts, and we have heard some of them mutter: 'Shut off that noise.'

Another factor common to almost all illnesses may influence the patients' responses to music: most of them cannot be attentive for a normal length of time. To exceed their limit of attention may destroy the benefit they could otherwise have gained from music. Our experience is that certain severely subnormal patients cannot sustain their attention on the same thing for more than twenty seconds, although this can be substantially increased with progressive techniques. Dr Newman, in the course of musical experiments with mental cases, has observed that his neurotic patients could barely tolerate or attend pieces of music of more than about four minutes' duration.[1]

Moreover, certain people suffering from physiological or psychological disorder have not developed at a normal rate. Many of them who are emotionally or mentally immature cannot function or progress at the usual pace. Some of them are unable to project themselves into the future. They need an immediate musical reward.

These two deficiencies may influence their responses to music. Music sessions based on a normal length or a normal rate of progress may fail with them, even when the musical activity is well geared to their personality.

Since the physical and the psychological responses react on one another, the number of non-measurable factors involved in the process makes music therapy an art more than a science.

But a scientific outlook has more or less prevailed in the case of physical ills, in the observation and assessment of the influence of music on physiological processes and functions. There, some distinction has been and is made between the emotional and the purely physical effect of music on man. In the next chapters we will attempt to separate the two aspects: one that is measurable according to rational or scientific investigation; the other which cannot be assessed by scientific terms.

The understanding of the nature and causes of man's responses to music is indispensable to the application of music therapy, since it aims at certain results which may require different

---

[1] Newman, *Symposium on Music Therapy, Tension and Relaxation*, paper published by the Society for Music Therapy and Remedial Music, London (1964).

techniques. One of its objects is to observe the patient's responses to certain musical experiences, responses that may be helpful to the diagnosis or to the treatment of the illness. Another of its objects is deliberately to provoke certain reactions, and then to control and channel them towards a specific therapeutic aim.

13. PSYCHOLOGICAL RESPONSES TO MUSIC
THE INDIVIDUAL

The responses to music which arise first from a perceptual stimulus are both psychological and physiological. Their reaction to one another produces a general effect related to the combination of diverse musical elements present in the same piece, for instance when melody and colour or rhythm and pitch are joined together. The same melody played on different instruments, or at different pitches, may provoke different reactions, and even sometimes of an opposite kind.

According to Combarieu, music has been used at all times as an offensive or a defensive means. Either it was used to provoke a pathological state, even of a contagious nature, or it was meant to remedy a disorder, calm the subject and bring him back to normal.[1]

We have already seen that music can induce morbid states, excite or relax them, a fact often found in the life of the prophets. Elishah said: 'But now bring me a minstrel'. And it came to pass, when the minstrel played, that the hand of the Lord came upon him.[2]

The psychological responses to a musical experience depend on the ability of the listener or the performer to communicate and to identify with it. This does not necessarily depend on the standard of the music or on the level of achievement of the musical performance. Imagery, association or self-expression to be found in music spring out of what is already in the individual,

[1] Combarieu, *La Musique et la Magie*, p. 86.
[2] 2 Kings iii.15.

which we have to discover, and is often revealed by the experience itself.

Music works at id, ego and superego levels. It can stir up or express primitive instincts and even help to let them loose— it can help to strengthen the ego, release and control the emotions at the same time, give a sense of purpose to the listener or the performer—it can sublimate certain emotions, satisfy the desire for perfection through high aesthetic and spiritual experiences. Music can express the whole range of man's experiences because of its relationship to the three levels of his personality.

Our growing knowledge of man's behaviour and of his responses to certain experiences enables us to understand better the meaning and the significance of his responses to music and to apply them therapeutically. We propose to discuss the main psychological effects of music on the individual which may result in communication, identification, association, imagery, self-expression and self-knowledge.

Communication

It is commonly stated that 'music is a means of communication'. In this simple truth lies the tremendous therapeutic value of music, since illness is the result of a breaking up of communication.

Man is a gregarious animal; he needs the presence of others to fulfil his physical and psychological needs; he has not been born to live in isolation. Moreover, his survival and development have always depended on his sense perception and his intelligence, which enable him to integrate with the world around him.

The tragedy of sickness is that it always creates isolation or insecurity, it impairs contacts and normal relationships with the environment. Many of the perceptual, mental or emotional processes through which man communicates with the world go wrong through an illness of mind or body.

We have already discussed how music has helped man from

primitive times to identify with his environment and to become aware of the forces at work around and within himself.

Identification

At any time and whatever his purpose the man who imitated and interpreted the sounds he heard became part of a world of sounds to which he gradually gave a realistic or a symbolic meaning. This applies equally well to the primitive man living in the jungle as to the modern pianist at the keyboard. Even when the sounds have become organised and purely symbolic, they may retain something of a realistic non-musical experience. Unexpected sound effects can be disquieting in music, as in a dark forest a mass of increasing sounds may feel as overpowering as the flow of a river.

Music expresses feelings arising from a situation and is not often imitative. Beethoven in his picture of 'the storm', however realistic it might have sounded, said explicitly that he had tried not to imitate but to express the feelings he had experienced during the storm. The listener in turn may go through the same feelings. Aristotle gives us a penetrating analysis of the process which we may relate to the Iso magic principle that 'like acts on like':

'And further when we listen to imitations we all acquire a sympathy with the feelings imitated even apart from actual rhythms and melodies. . . . But it is in rhythms and melodies that we have the most realistic imitations of anger and mildness as well as of courage, temperance and all their opposites of moral qualities generally. This we see from actual experience, as it is in listening to such imitations that we suffer a change within our own soul. But to acquire the habit of feeling pain or pleasure upon the occurrence of resemblances is closely allied to having the same feelings as in the presence of the real originals.'[1]

[1] Aristotle, *Politics*, Book V, p. 237.

In this case the 'originals' are the composer's own feelings and ideas. If the listener has never experienced them or if they are expressed in an idiom foreign to him, he will either not communicate or adopt his own interpretation related to his personal experiences.

This process takes place in a greater or less degree in any musical experience, in performer and listener alike. In the passage we have quoted Aristotle makes the pertinent remark that a habit must be acquired, which we may call today conditioning.

The function to which music is associated often helps to condition the listener to a certain mood, either receptive or adverse. This conditioning may happen suddenly or through a slow-forming habit. So is the slowly acquired response to the tone of the organ associated with church and religious feelings. On the other hand, in the story of Farinelli[1] the King's response to the music was immediate and reinforced by daily performances.

Man identifies himself with the music to which he can give his own interpretation. He can also identify with the composer if the music reflects the composer's personality or his life. Much music speaks of the composer as a man: Schumann described his schizophrenic tendencies in the dual portraits of Florestan and Eusebius; Smetana's 'quartet of my life' was his own biography in which even his tragic attack of deafness was realistically rendered by a long piercing note.

Music contains definite masculine and feminine characteristics which are present as well in any human being. Certain people feel attracted by the sexual ambivalence revealed in Tchaikovsky's or Brahms's music. Most music has a dominant masculine or feminine character. On the whole Beethoven's music expresses a virile personality; in Chopin's the feminine element is conspicuous.

[1] See pp. 63–66.

Music has sometimes expressed personality traits, without being necessarily a musical portrait. Haydn spoke of the 'moral characters' present in his music, which must have made some effect of sympathy or antipathy on the listener.[1]

The personal interpretation of the listener or of the performer amounts to an act of re-creation and can answer a need for creative activities. In some way the reaction of the listener depends on the personal interpretation of the performer. We may commonly speak of 'his Mozart' or 'her Scarlatti'.

Since music can express human characteristics in musical terms, it can also reveal some personality disorders. In an over-seas psychiatric social club I met a middle-aged patient who described to me in purely musical terms his search for his lost personality. He was a fairly good amateur pianist; could not read or write music, but had a talent for improvisation by ear. Each of his improvisations made musical sense.

He told me that the trouble resided in the fact that he could not find 'his own style'—style here meant personality. Every day, he said, he composed in a different style and this distressed him deeply. He had no record of the improvisations he made day after day, and went on trying to find his own self in music. We suggested a purely musical solution, namely that each of his impro-visations should be recorded and dated; then a number of them played back would help to find a centre, or a common denomina-tor among the various musical elements. This needed the help of a competent music therapist, able to interpret the result, and to make him to find his style.

Association

Music is part of so many functions and places, that every human being is exposed to it and in various ways; it is not only related to actual moods, but to past experiences. Man absorbs sounds,

[1] Alfred Einstein, *A Short History of Music*, p. 129.

often unconsciously, and retains music in his mind, perhaps even very short passages which can recall memories of facts, moods or feelings associated with it. Music can also recall perceptual sensations, such as smells, touch or colour.

The interviews given to various people in the B.B.C. 'Desert Island Discs' programme bring out the associative power of music. They reveal that many of its emotional effects are due to its association with people, friends or family and various life experiences. Rarely does the interviewee state that his choice is prompted by purely musical reasons.

The success or failure of music therapy depends on human as well as musical factors of relationship. An assessment of the patient's response to music should include what could be called his 'musical history'.

Personal musical experiences seem to leave a profound trace in the memory and may become associated with feelings of success or failure. Many people are more sensitive and vulnerable about music than about any other subject without being particularly musical. A great number of adults remember bitterly that as a child they were told that they were not musical, because they could not beat time or sing in tune, deficiencies that have nothing to do with a love of or a need for music, and which resulted in rejection. To be rejected from the choir seems to be a bitter experience, bitterly remembered for a long time. And then, music becomes associated with a painful event, and may in turn be rejected.

Even indirectly music can be a strong reminder of a failure or a success with which it has been associated. The following case may illustrate the point.

Norma was an intelligent, musical woman who suffered from an inferiority complex. She was persuaded that from the day she left school everything she did was inferior. She had abandoned her musical pursuits which had been very successful, and was now musically and emotionally blocked up. At our first music session she brought a melody which she had not sung since her last school concert. She told us how successful it had been, but was persuaded that she could never do it again. She had brought her own music to accompany herself. But with maturity her voice had gone down and she could not reach the high notes of the former key. After a few bars she broke down in a fit of sobbing, saying she had been right and could not do now what she had done so well in her schooldays.

We explained to her that the reason for this was a purely technical one, her voice was no more in the high register. The following week we provided her with a suitable version of the song and helped her to go through successfully to the end.

This musical success was of help towards her rehabilitation. It enabled her to relate the present to her musical past without a feeling of failure, and to gain self-confidence in the process.

If music can provoke associations with real life experiences, much of its evocative power is imaginary or extra-sensorial. Music made of elusive impalpable sounds can express a world of unreality and fantasy, of escape and dreams. Man has a need for such experiences that should be fulfilled when he is well balanced and able to distinguish between reality and unreality. But when his mental balance is impaired we may question the value to him of an escape from reality through music or any other means.

Imagination is one of the most creative faculties of man when it is kept within reasonable bounds. Since music is wordless there are few limits to its evocative and imaginative power. Daydreaming, imagery, mental flights into an invisible world have been part of the musical experiences of man and are non-intellectual.

Music can create mental imagery of many kinds: realistic, fanciful, dreamlike, fantastic, mystical or hallucinatory.

Music in the background provokes dreamlike moods, a mood

through which the individual can escape in an imaginary world, get lost or find himself. Mellers, who sees music become a more and more individual experience, suggests that inevitably the listeners 'will look to art as a means of escape; the kind of music they like is that which gives them fairly obvious opportunities for nostalgia or self-dramatisation; in fact it is not so much the music itself as the day-dreams it gives rise to'.[1]

The serious Chomet struck a lighter note when he said that 'music inspires the most agreeable fancies',[2] a thought expounded by others in different ways, for instance in the idea that musical activities lead 'to fantasy in which as in day-dreaming, wrapped in ourselves, we allow our imagination full play, regardless of the realities of our environment'.[3]

These fancies, fantasies and others most frequently evoke visual images. But they can also evoke secondary sensations such as colour. It has been stated that the relation between tone and colour is highly subjective and impossible to analyse. But James Mursell[4] is of the opinion that 'the arousal of colour sensation by tonal stimuli is not due to arbitrary associations and that it is not caused by happenings in the individual past experiences . . . it seems to be the result of the primary organisation of perceptual experience rather than of learning as ordinarily understood'.

The power of music to evoke images or sensations can explain its association with psychic states in which individuality, time and space disappear or take another dimension. Charles L. Myers suggests that music may consist in 'mystical experiences in which

---

[1] Wilfrid Mellers, *Music and Society*, Dennis Dobson, p. 13.

[2] D. H. Chomet, *The Influence of Music on Health and Life*, p. 223.

[3] Charles S. Myers, 'Individual Differences in Listening to Music', Max Schoen, *The effects of Music*, Pub. Kegan Paul & Co., London (1927), p. 36.

[4] James L. Mursell, *The Psychology of Music*, W. W. Norton & Co. Inc., New York (1937), p. 24.

we lose the normal awareness of our own individuality and its relation to our environment'.[1]

We find numerous historical references to mystical states induced by music. According to the esoteric philosophy of Hasidisia, 'songs without words could transform the soul of the singing worshipper to such an extent that definite stages of a mystic approach to God could be reached, stages which otherwise would have been most difficult to attain'.[2]

We hear of the strange charm which plunged the blessed Angela de Folingo (1309) into ecstasy when one day her soul was raised to the Uncreated Light while the organ was playing the Sanctus in the Church of St Francis.[3]

Certain listeners reach an ecstatic state for purely aesthetic reasons, which have nothing to do with religion. They seem to become lost in a world of beauty and emotion. We have seen children who were 'music struck' and motionless after listening to music. A performer may also experience a state of euphory in which the real world and even the audience seem to disappear.

If music can suppress the sense of space, it can also distort or obliterate the sense of time, without any mystical involvement, and in normal people. Experiments made in factories proved that the time seemed to pass more quickly when music was played. We also know that we may lose all sense of time—not, of course, the musical time—when playing or listening to music.

Music can provide a bridge between the real and the unreal, the conscious and the unconscious. This characteristic of music has been used in many situations. The lullaby helps the transition between wakefulness and sleep, or can bring to light a long-forgotten memory. It is not surprising that music has been

[1] Charles L. Myers, op. cit.

[2] Eric Werner, 'The Music of Post-Biblical Judaism', *New Oxford History of Music*, p. 333.

[3] *Theology of the Cross*, Cologne (1690), p. 328. Quoted by Yvonne Roskseth, *New Oxford History of Music*, Vol. III, p. 412.

associated with the world of dreams since primitive times. Healing music was often revealed to man in a dream and music was part of the dream-cures of illness.

We may be surprised that music has played only a small part in the analysis of dreams, and we have scarcely begun to observe the part that music could play in unconscious states. But the little amount of research made so far is highly significant, especially in cases of mental disorder. This will be discussed in the next chapter.

Music can provoke in the mind kinaesthetic images of movement that feel real. The listener to music may be like a sleeper in his dreams, and experience the feeling of performing physical actions. He may even live mentally certain experiences from sportive to erotic ones. Thus the process may be an imaginary substitute for action or movement.

Self-expression

Music which has the power to evoke, associate and integrate is for that reason an exceptional means of self-expression and emotional release. Suzanne Langer, who has studied the effects of music, recognises its power, but does not agree that emotional release is the primary function of music, even if, as she says, 'we use music to work off our subjective experiences and to restore our personal balance'.[1]

The primary function is not necessarily the most important. we may well believe that the highest function of music today is to give man an emotional outlet through an aesthetic experience adapted to his level of intelligence and education.

'An emotion is what moves us as the name implies', says Hadfield.[2] It comes from an accumulation of energy before dis-

[1] Suzanne K. Langer, *Philosophy in a New Key*, p. 217.
[2] J. A. Hadfield, *Psychology and Mental Health*, Unwin, 3rd edition (1960), p. 236.

charge. Emotion is a dynamic reaction to certain experiences and needs an outlet, since inhibition and repression are among the main sources of mental disorder. Moreover, emotions become conscious only when they have taken a form through some means of self-expression.

Music can answer the needs implied in these remarks. As a means of self-expression it brings into consciousness deep-seated emotions and provides the outlet necessary to their discharge; a function that music has fulfilled since time immemorial. The Greeks called the purging of the emotions the cathartic effect that some music made on the listener restoring him to a harmonious state.

Schneider, speaking of an even more distant past, suggests that 'music is the seat of secret forces or spirits which can be evoked by song in order to give man power which is either higher than himself or which allows him to rediscover his inner self'.[1]

Today as always the secret forces of music can help to reveal and awaken much of what is unexpressed or dormant in man. Sometimes it helps him to discover in himself a feeling for beauty, an unexpected ability or even a nostalgia. Aaron Copland suggests that 'great music awaken in us reactions of a spiritual order that are already in us, only waiting to be aroused'.[2]

If music can help the listener to explore and to discover his inner self through a deep psychological process, musical activities can help the performer to acquire or develop self-knowledge and knowledge of others through various means adapted to his personality. Whatever his level of ability or achievement, the performer functions in a world of positive action where he has to answer a challenge. He has to acquire some technical means of expression,

[1] Marius Schneider, 'Primitive Music', *New Oxford History of Music*, Vol. I, pp. 1–61.
[2] Aaron Copland, *Music and Imagination*, Mentor Books, U.S.A. (1959), p. 26.

to obey musical rules, to develop healthy interpersonal relationships, to behave in a socially acceptable way. The demands made on him, however slight, can help him to discover himself and others. Music-making is a shared experience which cannot be pursued or enjoyed without self-knowledge and an ability to communicate. This remark leads us to examine the influence of music on the group.

THE GROUP

If music has power on the mood and emotions of the individual, it exercises singular influence on the group. This characteristic is particularly interesting in view of the modern methods used in group therapy.

Mental health depends much on the balance between allegiance to a community and individual freedom of expression. The inability to conform to society and to find individual means of self-expression is one of the main symptoms of mental disturbance. The value of music in this case is that it can provide an emotional outlet within a group.

Music is the most social of all arts, which at all times has been a common experience. As part of a social function it has affected the man involved in it either as a participant or as a spectator. In itself music is a powerful integrating force to any function it accompanies by adding and giving to it a sense of order, time and continuity. Moreover, the sounds penetrating the group can be perceived by all, even if nothing can be seen. The result is that music can affect anyone in the group within hearing distance.

The herd instinct is ever present in the group and the effects of a musical experience are contagious. The group reacts to music as does the individual. Certain music provokes in the group harmony and orderly behaviour—other kinds incite a general lack of control and disorder.

4 MENTAL PATIENTS' ORCHESTRA

The late Dr Sydney Mitchell conducting his orchestra of patients in a psychiatric hospital

5 DANCING SESSION
IN A PSYCHIATRIC
HOSPITAL

6 MUSIC AND ART
(*left*) Picture inspired by
lively music and made by
a spastic child severely
deprived of movement

Very often, music expresses not the feeling of the individual but the feeling of a group. In primitive society, as Bowra suggests, music has expressed the tribal mind and has been to some extent the voice of a common consciousness'.[1] This has gone on throughout the ages and throughout the world. Music has been and still is the symbolic expression of a culture or the way of life of a group. Even today music, especially folkloric, may give man a feeling, perhaps nostalgic, of belonging to an ethnical group in the present or in the past. A national anthem is a symbol which belongs to all members of a national group, irrespective of their race, creed or political status within the group.

Music, being a non-verbal language, also possesses an international character. It has helped man to share and to communicate with other groups even when they belonged to other geographical communities. In spite of distance and language, man has used music as a means of communication with a wider world, far-away groups and their deeds. From Homer to the Minnesingers, from the minstrels and the troubadours to the modern string quartet, through the heroic song, the ballade or the broadcast performance, musicians have helped man to know about other men. Thus man has been able to build up little by little a musical inheritance common to many countries and many generations, which at the same time binds the past to the present.

Music has expressed the feelings of the group in communal functions in which the participants shared the same concern or the same interest. For instance, certain primitive healing rites involved the whole tribe, who gathered outside the sick man's hut, singing and playing sometimes for days and nights.

Music used in religious, stately or social gatherings usually affects or reflects the mood of the whole group. In Greek or Roman times as well as today various kinds of music festivals

---

[1] Bowra, *Primitive Song*, Weidenfield and Nicholson, p. 32.

and competitions gathered together music-lovers and others, irrespective of their social status. The fact that the pursuit of music cuts through social barriers has been and still is important to its influence on society.

Since music allows for individual freedom of expression within the control of a group we may conclude that such a group is an ideal means for group psychotherapy. It creates multifarious personal interrelationships between all its members, players, listeners and the music itself. Each member of the group has to accept a common discipline for the sake of something greater than any of them, namely the music. They have to behave musically and socially in an acceptable way. They have to tolerate one another, to feel free to criticise and to be criticised. Moreover, the music group in which everyone plays a part, as composer, listener or performer, according to his ability, answers man's fundamental desire to be needed and accepted by his fellow men.

14. PHYSICAL RESPONSES TO MUSIC

Observations and Measurements

It is not possible to measure scientifically the emotional effects of music, but since the initial impact of music is a physical one, we may be able to assess or even to measure the physiological responses to musical vibrations. This assessment might be of value to the application of music therapy.

We perceive sound through our auditory apparatus, whose nerves are set in motion and carry its effects through thalamic and cortical channels. But even without cortical involvement sound can arouse the activities of the autonomic nervous system.[1] We have already said that certain musical elements can provoke sensations at low brain level.

Some physical responses to music consist of spontaneous, un-

[1] *Therapeutic Notes* (Music and Medicine). Pub. Park, Davis & Co., London (1962), No. 4.

controllable reflexes. We may find ourselves unconsciously beating time when hearing music, or we suddenly notice that our breathing has become more rapid during an accelerating passage. These are involuntary reflexes.

Sometimes in the past the vibrations of musical sounds were supposed to act unconsciously on certain parts of the body affected by some disease. The process was then speculative and its use empirical. Today certain kinds of scientific apparatus enable us to measure the galvanic effects of musical vibrations on the skin, or to observe involuntary pupillary reflexes to a musical experience. Changes in skin resistance due to music have been tested through electrodes registering on a galvanometer the reactions of the listener. Podolsky[1] and Winold[2] agree that music can influence the electrical conductivity of the human body as manifested in these reflexes.

Certain musical elements already discussed definitely affect our nervous system. High or low pitch produces a corresponding effect of nervous tension or relaxation not always related to the general character of the music. The perception of abrupt contrasts, of sharp unexpected dissonances, requires a rapid adjustment of our auditory apparatus which may not react quickly enough. Exaggerated speed or volume can overstimulate the nerves and even produce a physically painful state.

In extreme cases, such as epilepsy, there may be a relation between music and the nervous discharge occurring during a fit. Hans H. Reese[3] has made a series of observations on epileptic patients and concludes in this way:

'We do not know the nature of the irritation or what

[1] E. Podolsky, *Music Therapy*, Philosophical Library, New York (1954), p. 157.
[2] Allen Winold, 'The Effects of Changes in Harmonic Tension on the Galvanic Skin Response', *MT* (1958), p. 188.
[3] 'Relation of Music to Diseases of the Brain', *MT*, ed. E. Podolsky, Philosophical Library, New York (1954), pp. 43-54.

unpleasant quality in the sound excites in some epileptics profound cortical discharges with obvious convulsive seizures. . . .
Musicogenic epilepsy is a term indicating that the association
between musical stimuli and an epileptic attack is close, and that
epileptic seizures are precipitated only by specifically irritating
music. . . . Cases of musicogenic epilepsy are very rare.' He
concludes the description of several cases in saying: 'If this
concept is correct musicogenic epilepsy should be regarded as a
highly integrated form of reflex epilepsy due to sensory irritation
rather than as an example of psychic precipitation of the seizures
alone.'

The emotional impact of music, however slight, may provoke
certain involuntary physiological responses, such as changes in
the rate or evenness of blood circulation, or in the breathing
process. Already in antique Alexandria a famous physician had
noticed certain effects of music on his pulse rate. Another
medical man, P. J. Buchoz, wrote in 1769 a serious book on his
original method to test his patients' pulse through music.[1] The
composer Grétry made some experiments on himself on these
reactions to music.

Since scientific apparatus can measure cardiac and respiratory
activity, some physicians have been able to observe the effect of
selected music on respiratory or heart rate. E. Podolsky,[2]
Douglas Ellis and Gilbert Brighouse[3] have made various experiments on changes in the heart rate produced by music. The heart
is an organ whose function is deeply affected by emotional factors,
factors which are not easily measurable.

The patterns of musical rhythms and sequences are closely

[1] E. Ashworth Underwood, 'Apollo and Terpsichore', *Bulletin of the
History of Medicine*, Vol. XXI, No. 5, September–October 1947, pp. 639–73.
[2] E. Podolsky, 'Effects of Music on the Heart', pp. 155–7.
[3] Douglas Ellis and Gilbert Brighouse, 'The Effects of Music on Respiratory and Heart Rate', in *MT*, ed. E. Podolsky, Philosophical Library,
New York (1954), pp. 158–69.

allied to certain physical functions. There is in music as well as in any living body a perceptible alternation of tension and relaxation, of activity and repose, which exists even in the vibrations of a single sound.

Rhythmical patterns and melodic lines in music correspond closely to similar characteristics in man's body—they do not only reflect emotional or mental life, which Aristotle described as imitations or resemblances. Suzan Langer[1] has described perfectly the resemblance between music and man's physical and mental rhythm when she writes that:

'. . . there are certain aspects of the so-called "inner life"— physical or mental—which have formal properties similar to those of music—patterns of motion and rest, of tension and release, of agreement and disagreement, preparation, fulfilment, excitation, sudden changes, etc. . . .'

The correlation between musical and innate bodily rhythm has been stressed by many writers. Alfred Einstein suggests that 'the practice of music among primitive people shows a continual movement between two opposite extremes, excitement and repose'.[2]

Thayer Gaston is more positive when he sees in music a means of generating physical strength. He has made an extensive study of the dynamic factors in music, especially rhythm 'which stimulates muscular action and induces bodily action. Certain primitive dances such as the African war dances enhance and build up physical energy.'[3]

Emotional involvement is not always necessary for music to affect or help some purely physical activity. This happens, for instance, in circus acrobatics or in gymnastics. Rhythmical patterns combined with a melody, namely a series of movements

[1] Suzan K. Langer, *Philosophy in a New Key*, p. 228.
[2] Alfred Einstein, *Short History of Music*, p. 2.
[3] Thayer Gaston, *Music Educators Journal*, February–March 1951.

in sounds, have been through the ages a means of alleviating physical fatigue. From time immemorial music has accompanied hard physical tasks in the life of slaves, convicts, sailors and many others. Even a simple melodic line by itself may contain enough dynamism to be used in physical culture. We are told that in ancient Greece 'One or several players of aulos or flute were on the staff of each "palestre". Their task was to give rhythm to all the physical exercises, not only the gymnastic, but also the throwing of the disc, or of the javelin and other games.'[1]

Singing or playing an instrument makes physical demands on the performer, sometimes exacting ones. Its effect on the performer can be medically tested, measured and controlled.

Singing has at all times been thought beneficial to respiratory and even digestive functions, and may affect man's whole physical health. It may even be a treatment in itself.

Man's body can be considered as a resonant as well as a rhythmical instrument, sensitive to music. The musical instruments he has invented are in essence a prolongation of his own body and activated by his physical impulses. His body and his instrument are not separate entities, they complete one another. This characteristic enables the player to identify physically with his instrument through a perceptual contact which is indispensable to create an emotional response. Irrespective of the emotional motivation behind it, singing or playing a musical instrument is a physical process. It requires the use of muscular and motor control, and spatial judgement. At even the lowest level it demands some auditory and tactile perception without which there cannot be any emotional outlet.

The physiological effects of music on the listener or the performer are measurable, even when some emotional factors are present. It may be regrettable that, on the whole, we tend to pass

[1] R. Flaceliere, *La Vie Quotidienne en Grece du Temps de Pericles*, Hachette, Paris, p. 133. Author's translation.

by or to ignore many of the physical reactions to music, especially those which are subtle and not very obvious. We chiefly watch and wait for the emotional response of the patient. Nevertheless in the treatment of a physical illness or handicap our concern should first be for the body in distress, which needs relief and cure.

IV

The Practice of Music Therapy

INTRODUCTION

MUSIC therapy has become a more or less recognised ancillary therapy and a remedial means. Today a number of physicians, psychologists, educationists and musicians are taking an interest in the subject. Some of them have made valuable research especially in the United States, where music therapy is a profession with a training and a recognised status. But, however original and interesting, many of these experiments have not been followed up and led to their clinical application. For instance, the excellent research made by Dr Schneider[1] on the opposite response of spastic and athetoid subjects on rhythm and melody does not seem to have been continued and its results applied. The same remark can be made of the study undertaken by Sommer[2] on certain distorted auditory perceptions she had observed in schizophrenics, although further investigations might have had some use in the medical diagnosis of the illness or in its treatment.

Certain data is neglected in many cases. There are hospitals where the musical history of the patient is not taken down at the time of his admission, although such information is vital to the application of music therapy.

[1] Dr Edwin Schneider, 'Relationship between Musical Experiences and Certain Aspects of Cerebral Palsied Children's Performance', *MT* (1956), p. 250.
[2] D. T. Sommer, 'Music in the Autobiography of Mental Patients', unpublished paper (1960).

There seems to be a need for integration between the various aspects of the subject, and a lack of communication between its many exponents. More cohesion is indispensable if music therapy is to become a real subject or even a discipline of its own.

In this book we are attempting to make a synthesis of the copious but scattered material known to us. This attempt is based on our personal experience in most fields of music therapy and on our own knowledge of the work of many other exponents. This synthesis may not be as complete as we wish it to be, but we hope that an integrated book of this kind will be followed by others which could endeavour to fill the gaps left in our study of the contemporary scene.

Our synthesis attempts to include the application, study and experiments recently made in different countries not only by physicians and psychologists but also by fully experienced musicians equipped with the necessary psychological and medical understanding, people whose attitude and work is of the highest standard. If some of their opinions seem controversial, that should not detract from the value of their research.

15. MUSIC IN THE TREATMENT OF PHYSICAL DISORDER

In spite of popular belief, music therapy is not concerned only with disorders of the mind. Since music affects man's body, it can be of value in the treatment of physical illness or disability.

Although history shows us that for a long time man has observed the influence of music on physiological functions, in the modern era there has been very little research done on its application in the treatment of physical illness. In consequence this chapter, concerned only with the contemporary application of music therapy in the physical field, is necessarily short.

Many physiological disorders or infirmities result in a lack of physical contacts with the environment or in a disability of movement more or less severe which impairs life in various ways and degrees. Among them are brain damage, cerebral palsy, polio, muscular distrophy, respiratory diseases and also sensory handicaps such as blindness or deafness. There are also congenital or accidental infirmities. When the handicap is not curable, the patient maimed for life may be facing psychological difficulties. He often needs some help to acquire the right attitude towards his disability. Some patients may be hopeful or pessimistic, resigned or revolted, some withdraw, others stiffen up. The treatment of such maladjustments goes hand in hand with the physical treatment dealing with the cause of the handicap.

Many physical illnesses or injuries result in partial or severe paralysis, or in deficiences in motor control and spatial judgement. The treatment of such disorders, among other things, aims at giving the patient as many perceptual contacts as possible with the world, at developing or rehabilitating his muscular strength and co-ordination. Physiotherapy plays a major part in the treatment of such disorders, to which music can be of real assistance.

We have seen that listening to or making music can act as a stimulus and a regulator of movement, and that rhythm or other dynamic elements provoke spontaneous physical reflexes. The patient who suffers from defective muscular co-ordination and a lack of physical rhythm can be helped by the dynamism of music when he tries to find or re-create in himself a sense of orderly rhythm without which his movements and even his speech may be disorderly and uncontrolled. In such cases listening to and making music are two processes complementary to one another.

The technique of musical instruments which are hit or shaken can help him to direct a specific movement in space and in time. The manipulative process which gives concrete perceptual contact with an instrument is in many cases highly therapeutic. Musical instruments can be adapted to the kind of physical or mental state of the patient, as is done with objects such as furniture or tools used by the patient at home, in the school, or with the industrial equipment he uses in the workshop.

We can relate the technique of a musical instrument to the manual training undertaken in a workshop. In music-making or at the bench we use similar movements, for instance grasping a tool, hitting at a specific place and then relaxing the muscles. The process should produce in the patient the feeling of alternating tension and relaxation necessary to start and to complete the movement. Moreover, the patient may be helped to form in his mind a picture of the movement producing the musical sound he is expecting to hear, a mental process the physiotherapeutic treatment tries to develop.

Dr Sidney Licht advocates the practice of certain instruments, the technique of which can help to develop specific muscles. He recommends the piano, which offers excellent opportunities for flexion of the fingers and thumb, extension, abduction of the wrist as well as flexion and abduction of the shoulders and exercise of the neck and back. Violin or cello technique develops the flexibility of the left fingers, the flexion and extension of the right elbow and of the wrist, the abduction and adduction of the shoulder.[1]

Music plays a great part in the special education of brain-damaged and other physically affected children and adults. Its value to such cases is recognised in a great number of countries by physicians as well as educationists. It is therefore surprising that so little research has been done on its purely physiological aspects. Beatrice Fields's experiment has been one of the first in 1955. She made a three-year study on the use of music and musical activities in treatment directed towards an increase in motor co-ordination with twenty-eight severely disabled brain-damaged patients. The patients ranged in age from fifteen to fifty-four years and presented neurological symptoms of spasticity,

[1] From Dr S. Licht, *Music in Medicine*, New England Conservatory of Music (1946), pp. 48–53.

athetosis, rigidity, ataxia, tremor and associated speech, auditory and visual defects.

The treatment employed consisted of patient participation in simple instrument and piano-keyboard activities. Measurable improvement in both gross and fine motor co-ordination in twenty-four out of the twenty-eight patients was noted. Such improvement in motor co-ordination also was observed to carry over into other activities. These findings were considered to be specifically significant with seven of the patients, because other therapy activities with these patients had either been terminated or confined to activities not in any way related to those used in the experimentation.[1]

In this experiment ordinary musical instruments were used and found suitable. But there exist a few others specially devised for use in orthopaedics as a help towards physical rehabilitation of the muscles. There are pedal-operated maracas; the British Faulkner dulcichord, a keyboard instrument which can be tilted down for the use of reclining patients in bed; the American clinic organ described by Soibelman.[2] We can also find a number of devices or gadgets invented to enable physically handicapped patients to use normal instruments. For instance, a piano-pedal gadget working mechanically or electrically from pressure from the back for paraplegic patients; or special attachments enabling spastics to hit the keys with an apparatus fixed on the forehead, a technique already used in typewriting by patients who have lost the use of arms and hands.[3] Special prostheses[4] have been

[1] Beatrice Fields, 'Music as an Adjunct in the Treatment of Brain-Damaged Patients', American Journal of Physical Medicine, 33–35, October 1954, pp. 273–83. Quoted by Edwin H. Schneider, PH.D., in 'Music Therapy Research for Physically Handicapped', MT (1955), pp. 183–8.

[2] Doris Soibelman, Therapeutic and Industrial Uses of Music, Columbia University Press (1948), p. 152.

[3] Vally Weigl Keyboard, New York.

[4] Devised by the House of Bidwell Inc., Milwaukee.

devised to fit the needs of the handicapped: an artificial hand or arm can enable a cripple to play the piano; its extensible controllable fingers can even play triads or other chords; an orthopaedic hand can be made to hold and move a bow across the strings.[1]

With the help of such devices the practice of certain instruments can be a real physical therapy, irrespective of the musical standard of the patient.

A therapist who has worked with a number of physically handicapped patients quotes the case of a young girl with whom she worked for several years and achieved extremely good results. The six-year-old girl was referred to her for music therapy. The patient suffered from a congenital loss of the left hand and was prescribed piano lessons as a means towards physical rehabilitation. The girl, who was musical, was made first to practise only with her right hand. Then she was fitted with a prosthesis specially made which enabled her to play the piano and she attained quite a good standard after a few years.

The study provoked physical growth in several directions: it helped to strengthen the patient's left arm and shoulder and enabled her to use muscles which otherwise might have become weaker and atrophied. It also helped her not to overload her right arm and shoulder. Her piano-playing taught her to use her prosthesis better and to control the muscles involved in motion, pronation and supination. These various processes proved to be an effective means of physical therapy, irrespective of the deep psychological effect it had on her whole life.[2]

The most striking case we have seen among many others was a boy of twelve born without legs. He had two normal arms, but

---

[1] Sister M. Josepha, O.S.F., Alverno College, 'The Therapeutic Value of Instrumental Performance for Severely Handicapped Children', *Journal of Music Therapy*, Vol. I, No. 3, pp. 73–79.

[2] Sister M. Josepha, op. cit.

the right hand was missing and replaced by an orthopaedic hook. His only hand was a shapeless stump with two fingers. In spite of this appalling handicap he was of average intelligence, very sociable and had a lovely sensitive face. Music had become the centre of his life. He had learned the trumpet, the only instrument he could manage, holding it with the hook and pressing on the keys with his fingers. His teacher helped him to develop an uncanny physical skill, using control of movement in time and space, and achieving a really good standard of playing.[1]

Another case: John McKee, born with spastic limbs, describes in his autobiography how music helped him to develop the physical skill and strength of his spastic hand in playing the drum:

'My drumming resulted from not being able to play the clarinet . . . for a long time my left hand did all the work . . . with practice however my right hand became more useful and drumming gave that spastic hand more strength and direction than it had ever before . . . my right hand became responsive enough so that I could get a satisfactory roll out of a drum.'[2]

Certain physical illnesses, such as muscular distrophy, are not curable; the patient suffers from creeping paralysis and is more and more crippled. A therapist[3] who worked with hopeless victims of such disease is of the opinion that music can help them in a general way, and perhaps even physically. She believes that with patients suffering from physical disabilities it is difficult to know how much they are helped physically by a programme of musical activities. Her techniques enable the child to act himself and use all the ability he possesses without being helped.

---

[1] J. Alvin, *Music for the Handicapped Child*, O.U.P. (1965), pp. 123-4.

[2] John D. McKee, *Two Legs to Stand On*, Appleton Century Crofts Inc., New York, p. 76.

[3] Frances Korson, 'Music Therapy for Children with Muscular Distrophy', *MT* (1957), pp. 192-4.

She thinks that the movements involved might be an influence in counteracting disuse atrophy and in slowing down the progress of paralysis.

Orthodontics

A number of ancient texts tell us that Alcibiades and Athanea both rejected the flute because it disfigured their countenance. Today we are told by experts that the playing of wind instruments can be an aid to orthodontics and even improve the appearance of people suffering from malformation of the mouth. Two Cleveland specialists, a dental surgeon and a trumpeter, have made a joint study of the therapeutic value of wind instruments, namely when the treatment requires the strengthening of the lips and mouth muscles. They state that 'when the patient has a short hypotoned upper lip, a flabby lower lip and a protrusive tongue, trumpet playing will both strengthen the lips and confine tongue action within a definite area. . . .' They also add that 'the deep regular breathing required when playing a trumpet will tend to improve the breathing function.'[1]

Wilhelmina Harbert had described a difficult case for which she used the dynamics of vocal production. The medical diagnosis indicated paralysis of throat muscles; thrombosis, right cerebellar artery; hemiparesis of pharyngeal extrinsic muscles; vocal chords intact. The patient was a young man. He had no musical history and was a non-singer, but willing to try. His physical state was distressing. He communicated only in aspirated breathy sounds, had no abdominal muscular support for breathing, and experienced difficulty in swallowing his saliva.

The therapist to whom the patient was referred by his doctor used various means to help vocal production, which followed slow

[1] Howard E. Kessler, D.D.S., and Aloys Hruby, 'Dentistry and the Musical Wind Instrument Problem', in *Dental Radiography and Photography*, Vol. 32, No. 1 (1959), pp. 1–8.

gradual stages: a harmonica to gain control over inspiration and expiration of breath; exercises on vowels, consonants and words spoken on different pitches and notes; rotative exercises of the head and neck to music, followed by other physical movements to music, such as walking or clapping.

The patient's vocal ability increased gradually in control, pitch and rhythm. He began to be able to read to music spoken sentences of increasing length. After a year's gradual treatment his vocal range, his articulation and inflexion of voice were satisfactory enough. His timbre was coarse and rough with a nasal chest and throat resonance, but his speaking ability had been restored, and he had acquired a singing ability. Through the process, he had regained stability and confidence in himself.[1]

Singing has always been recognised as beneficial to certain physiological functions such as breathing, and remedial in the case of their disturbance. A number of early observations made by physicians on the value of singing were related to its physiological effects on the singer. Richard Browne[2] had already recommended singing in cases of respiratory diseases, but with a certain discrimination, which seemed to be logical. His initiative does not seem to have been followed up by modern physicians. But some musicians, especially singing teachers, have observed the good effect of singing on the physical state of some of their pupils and have even studied it under medical guidance.

In Great Britain and other countries where choral music is flourishing, a number of educationists concerned with the health of handicapped pupils advocate singing as a therapeutic means against certain physical ailments. In a paper on backward children, J. P. B. Dobbs speaks of some of the physical chronic disabilities many of these children suffer from, namely adenoids and

[1] Wilhelmina K. Harbert, 'Music Technique applied in Disordered Speech', *MT* (1953), p. 59.
[2] See p. 55.

catarrhal troubles which affect their breathing and hearing. He has noticed that 'the breathing of subnormal children is often shallow and badly controlled. . . . Their general health will improve as a result of the regular systematic training in deep breathing and breath control required in singing.'[1]

The preceding quotations refer only to the physiological processes involved in singing or playing a musical instrument, and not to the emotional impact of musical activities on the patient. Perhaps, without going as far as the emotions, we should agree that the use of a musical instrument cannot be entirely mechanical. The keyboard of a piano, even considered as a means of physical therapy, conveys a different meaning from that of a typewriter; exercises done to music lose their dreariness and take on certain significance even when they are not more than physical training and are not meant to be a means of self-expression.

The support that music gives to a purely physical activity has already been discussed. Most physiotherapists agree that music accompanying remedial exercises enables the most un-musical patient to function better and longer. Musical rhythm stimulates bodily action; it has always been known to alleviate physical fatigue in the listener and the performer alike. Even when the music played during physical exercises is musically insignificant, it has form, a harmonic and melodic temporal continuity, elements which give meaning to repetitive, inex-pressive movements.

This effect of music is noticeable when it accompanies the repetition of certain sounds that would otherwise feel static and might breed boredom, fatigue or inattention. The verbal sounds seem to be moving with the music on a sequence of chords that develop musically towards a logical conclusion. Some musicians

[1] *Music and Backward Children*, paper published by the Society for Music Therapy and Remedial Music, London (1960), read at the Conference, Music Therapy in the Education of the Child, London, 1960.

have used this technique as a help in the treatment of speech defects.[1]

In a strict medical sense the word therapy should be used only in connection with the curative treatment of an illness. We may well ask if the term can apply when the patient is not curable, or when his infirmity is not an illness. Quite often there is no rehabilitation, but habilitation, or the means used are compensatory, not remedial.

When the incurable suffers from emotional or social maladjustment, then music can offer unique therapeutic means which will be described in the following chapter. But before discussing the psychological effect of music on people suffering from a sensory infirmity, such as blindness or deafness, we can observe its value in the development of compensatory means. The compensatory means used in the remedial education of such patients do not affect their disability, but offer them other avenues of growth. This aspect may be outside the scope of this book, but we have developed it fully elsewhere.[2]

At the purely sensory level, the use of music can help the blind to develop auditory perception and teach him to rely on his power of listening to sequences of sound. Moreover, the use of music in his physical training may help him to develop the spatial sense he is lacking.

With the deaf, music can be physically therapeutic, because it corrects certain physiological defects due to the infirmity. The deaf child misses bodily rhythm which comes from hearing. A normal child absorbs rhythm naturally through the various noises surrounding him from birth. He instinctively feels them as rhythm patterns to which his body responds, a fact which applies to all physical movements, including those involved in speech. A deaf child, unconscious of an inner physical rhythm,

[1] John A. Harvey, *Articulation and Activity Songs*, Paxton & Co., London.
[2] J. Alvin, op. cit., p. 19.

may walk or speak in a chaotic way. Ludin tells us that 'rhythm must be correlated with some internal mechanism for the impression of rhythm to arise".[1]

The fact that some modern methods for teaching the deaf include music seems to be paradoxical. But music then is used in a simple form of rhythmical vibrations. The child perceives them through nervous channels other than the auditory ones, through his skin and his bones. The sound vibrations can be transmitted to the child through resonant bodies such as the wooden floor on which he is dancing, or the skin of the drum he is playing, or the side of the piano on which he is leaning. Then he is able to apprehend the vibrations, to feel and to memorize their rhythmical pattern. He learns how to use them in his speech as well as in his physical movements, even in dancing. This method, which promotes health of body and mind, has been applied in Britain and other countries for some time. It is medically recommended by specialists in this country and others, such as the Netherlands.

Although it is necessary and possible to a certain extent to assess the value of music in the treatment of physical disorders, and whether we call it remedial, compensatory or therapeutic, the effects of music never stop there. A musical experience integrates the whole man and in one operation involves his body, mind and emotions.[2]

16. MUSIC IN THE TREATMENT OF MENTAL ILLNESS

Recreation and Therapy

The most obvious and easy application of music in therapy is recreation. We admit that many specialists would not call recreation a real therapy even if the results are beneficial. The

[1] Robert W. Ludin, *An Objective Psychology of Music*, The Ronald Press Co., New York (1953).

[2] J. Alvin, *Musical Theory and Instrumental Technique*, Augener.

therapeutic results of recreational music depend on the skill of the music therapist and on the size and nature of the group for which a common denominator has to be found. In a large group, the generalised use of music may diminish its effects on the individual.

This may be the place to mention that music therapy should not be considered as a kind of occupational therapy. Both are creative and recreative, but even if some of their principles of application seem to be similar, music therapy works fundamentally on effects of and responses to sound and on everything that is involved in a musical experience. The two therapies may be complementary to one another, but they work on different conceptions. We have seen recently an occupational therapist trying to communicate with a very severely retarded blind child. She put in his hands small musical instruments easy to manipulate, helped the child to feel and to explore their shape. Only then did she make the boy strum the string of the psaltery and hit the cymbals. The tone he produced was weak. Since an occupational therapist is mostly concerned with the shape and the making of objects, it was normal for her to wake up the awareness of the boy through touching the instruments before making him conscious of their sound.

A music therapist would have worked in the reverse way. She would have tried to communicate first through a well-produced resonant sound, and then made him touch the instrument which had caused the sound. Communication would have been established through the child's auditory perception reinforced by touch.

The Group

Music used as recreation usually consists of activities involving groups of different sizes, from two to a great number of listeners or performers. The temptation is often irresistible for any medical or educational organisation to cater for a number as large as possible, especially in music. This is a mistake, since the beneficial results we may expect when working with a group below fifteen become so diluted in a larger group that the activity may not amount to much more than a pleasant way of filling time. The therapist may lose the opportunity of watching and following individual behaviour and progress on which further work depends. This situation is even more regrettable with a short-term patient, who should be given the opportunity to integrate with a group as quickly as possible and may, for some time, feel lost or anxious in a large group, where he gets little personal attention.

Moreover, the music therapist working with a large group of patients is likely to become physically and nervously exhausted, since he has to project his personality and try to establish communication with each of the members. We have frequently observed this situation when the music therapist plays to or conducts a group of apathetic, regressed, agitated or volatile patients, whether adults or children. In that case, many therapists prefer to use recorded music and keep it at the level of general entertainment.

Some institutions plan a complete music-therapy programme, including recreational, educational and social activities, as well as individual therapy, each of them aiming at specific results. The late Dr Mitchell[1] expressed his opinion on recreational music, based on several years' experiments with music at Warlingham Park Mental Hospital:

'Entertainment, recreational and educational aspects of music were first in the foreground. . . . As others have observed, mixed programmes were most appreciated and produced temporary beneficial effects on mood. . . . We would like to

1 Dr Sydney D. Mitchell, M.D., M.B., D.P.M., 'Music in Mental Hospitals', *The Hospital*, October 1948.

emphasise that these forms of approach can hardly be called *specific* Musical Therapy.'

Recreation is in essence a way of passing the time in a leisurely, pleasant fashion and which does not entail an obligation or an effort which is not voluntarily accepted. In this chapter we propose to use the word 'recreation' in the strictly limited sense of an uncritical spontaneous pleasure of the moment involving no effort towards the acquisition or the improvement of musical skill and no projection towards the future. Such a narrow and arbitrary definition is scarcely acceptable, but it will help us to follow the stages through which recreation gradually becomes therapeutic and then may contribute to the medical treatment. This occurs when music becomes a means of self-expression, when it is applied to the control of behaviour, when it leads to self-knowledge and the knowledge of others.

In a recreational programme music is to the listener or the performer a source of conscious enjoyment. This process has nothing to do with the effect of background music which goes on when we may be otherwise occupied. Background music operates below conscious level; it performs a function other than being in itself an agreeable pastime.

We have already seen that the effects of music have always been bound to its function and depended on the conditions under which it was used. Music used as recreation, even in a therapeutic setting, can create or transform an atmosphere, for instance in a ward, enlivened at once by some kind of musical activity such as singing, playing, dancing or listening to live music.

Musical Equipment

Nevertheless, physical surroundings may enhance, spoil or distort the character of a musical experience. The environment may create a feeling of intimacy or prestige, of formality or ease, which are a help or a hindrance to the therapeutic effect.

Acoustics, too, play a part in the results. We recently visited a new centre for spastics where the play room was a concrete building so resonant that the children were deafened by the music, however softly it was played.

The use of mechanical devices to record or amplify the patients' performances makes a deep psychological effect on them. The sound of their own recorded or magnified voices is a great fillip to their ego.

Even with adults or children who do not seem to possess musical discrimination or ability, the material used for music therapy should be of a high standard, for musical and psychological reasons. Sound acts on the nerves which may be more sensitive in certain states of tension or irritability. The instruments have to be in tune and of the same pitch to produce a harmonious, pleasing tone. Tapes and records producing a rough or noisy tone are likely to produce rough and noisy responses. They are acceptable only if such responses are desired.

A good music library of sheet music and records, well chosen for its musical and therapeutic use, varied, adaptable and up to date, is indispensable to the music therapist; a suitable music room, good instruments and mechanical devices—all these are the basic tools of the music therapist. They should be as good as tools used in any other therapies. The standard of the equipment reflects the attitude of the administration responsible for it.

The budget of a music department should be well balanced to provide for the essentials, including the first of them, the therapists' remuneration. Too often the money is found for expensive tools and the vital human factor is forgotten, a situation we have found in a number of institutions.

The type of recreational music used depends on the tools available and on other amenities, although ultimately the results come from the way the music therapist handles the situation. Musical activities can be undertaken in various surroundings, in the wards, in a special music room, or even in the garden. The best results seem to occur when informality and a minimum of control create an atmosphere of ease. The seats disposed loosely in a circle or semicircle appear much less stiff and formal than arranged in straight rows. The musical instrument producing live or recorded music contributes better towards the integration of the group when it is placed in the middle of the circle; it serves as a uniting focal point. It may even give the small group a homely feeling in a situation that resembles the gathering of the tribe around the communal fire which gave life.

The most beneficial music sessions are those with short and varied items in order to avoid an impression of monotony and to fight against the boredom or fatigue that many hospital patients suffer from. A non-selected group is usually non-discriminating. Most of the listeners prefer music with simple harmonies, with catchy tunes they can remember, vocal operatic items and so on. They may also enjoy evocative or sensuous music which creates a general mood and may provoke imagery.

An experienced therapist does not plan the listening pro-gramme ahead, but tries to catch the mood of the group at the beginning and plays music reflecting that mood. Thus he can reach the listeners at once and, if desirable, works from the one mood towards other feelings.

Listening to music may lead some patients to want a more active form of participation. We can observe some of them beating the time spontaneously or humming the tune. From our own experience the best musical activities which can be pursued on purely recreational terms are singing or moving to music. These can be undertaken at the actual standard of the participant and need no effort. Most patients at some time have done school, community or church singing and are familiar with some tunes. Without much of a voice even a shy patient can try to hum in a vocal group which affords a feeling of protection.

Sing-song, popular community singing, but usually not hymns, prove to be the best repertoire for informal, spontaneous singing, in which note reading or part singing is not specially required. This kind of musical activity is invaluable in a psychiatric social club where members come and go and are often unable or unwilling to make an effort. The floating attendance makes very difficult any programme geared to the future. But the new-comer can be accepted right away as he is, if he first stands in the group and sings with them.

Dancing, or rather moving to music, spontaneously and as it comes, can be purely recreational. It involves no effort towards improvement. So does the use of certain rudimentary instruments which require no training at all. Both can be enjoyed at the same time.

These forms of spontaneous and undirected enjoyment are used in many hospitals with adults and children suffering from mental or emotional disorders. With physically affected patients it is not always easy to work spontaneously, and the use of instruments may have to be supervised with each individual. Moving to music, without any formal step, can gradually become a means of self-expression, sometimes unconscious. Some of the patients we can observe in the picture (Plate 5) have become involved and wrapped in themselves. Others have found a means of communication with a partner of the other sex. In both cases recreation has led to a deeper experience and become therapeutic. The music therapist who observes and follows these developments can help them to grow and benefit the patient.

Spontaneous enjoyment, entailing no effort or discrimination, is very popular with patients whose mind has lost or never possessed the power to criticise or discriminate. Generally speaking, these are geriatric or subnormal cases. These patients are not curable, there is no way out of senility or severe retardation, although psychiatric treatment can help the neurotic or the disturbed ones. But the use of simple music with them can make all the difference to their day-to-day happiness or well-being. The obvious pleasure and joy they experience in musical activities kept at their level are very rewarding to the music therapist. Musical enjoyment can help to stimulate their mind, revive old memories and activate their body. It lights a brief spark in a hopelessly dull and grey life. Many of these patients possess little self-respect. Standing up and singing for pleasure alone may give them, even for a short moment, a sense of dignity, since they partake in an activity which is neither material nor utilitarian.

If the purely recreational use of music is harmless, the music therapist should handle with caution any deeper reactions that go further than entertainment. Whatever the causes of the illness, patients suffering from mental, emotional or even physical disability are people who have failed and lost their self-confidence. They are vulnerable. Music can offer them an opportunity to succeed or even to vindicate themselves, if they can be persuaded to make an effort towards a specific aim. This effort involves a personal commitment, however brief or temporary. The patient should experience a feeling of immediate or near-at-hand success. Whatever his kind of illness, a patient is always a diminished person, whose interest and attention are difficult to sustain. The music therapist has to find ways of provoking and renewing the right motivation through musical means which, however unorthodox, can bring results.

Group Dynamics

In a number of hospitals and even in some special schools, music is mostly used as a means of recreation and entertainment. The musician in charge is not meant or able to attempt more, and this for several reasons.

We often meet the widespread belief that a large music group functions as well as a smaller one. This cannot apply to sick people whose power of attention is poor or diminished, although we often find that a greater number of patients are gathered together for music than for any other form of activity: indeed, music is sometimes used as a practical way of relieving a member of the staff whose group joins another one to make or listen to music. We also meet the belief that music cannot work at a deeper level than that of an enjoyable activity. We also meet, among musicians, much ignorance about the therapeutic value of music and a disbelief in the necessity for training and acquiring some medical or psychological knowledge.

In spite of its special value and interest, music therapy with individual patients still remains an exception. But the new techniques based on group dynamics are opening a wide door to their application to music group therapy. The group offers an opportunity to observe individual and group reactions and inter-personal relationships within a collective musical experience. The group consists of patients who suffer from different kinds or degrees of illness, but have a problem in common: loneliness and maladjustment.

Whatever its nature, illness isolates the patient and at the same time threatens his identity, especially when he is hospital-ised or when his illness depersonalises him. A music group gives him an opportunity to assert himself through the part he is responsible for, and at the same time to belong to a group where he is accepted.

Except in composing, music can provoke an infinite number and variety of human relationships which are more or less sub-jective. Rudolf Dreikurs has written some significant pages on group dynamics in music from which we extract the following passage:

'Musical experiences are usually not solitary, but occur in a group setting. We can well say that music and the group belong together. As music links people together and creates a group feeling, so the group seeks expression through music. The stronger the group is integrated, the more it makes of music, as in religious and political activities.

'The relationship between music and the group deserves closer scrutiny. It is too much taken for granted, so that the underlying dynamics are often overlooked. They certainly are not sufficiently considered . . . even in the use of music for therapeutic purposes.'[1]

In the musical situation, we can easily observe the reaction of the patient to the group, and of the group to the patient. These reactions reveal problems due to unresolved or unsatisfactory personal relationships. In the music group these relationships can be directed, corrected or relieved in various ways. Emotional disturbance, deviant personality or mental illness produce the same inability to relate to one's environment and to form harmonious human relationships. A music group therapeutically oriented can help the patient to communicate with individuals, to integrate with a group and to experience a feeling of belonging.

This can be achieved through a gradual transition from the one-to-one relationship to the integration with a group. The stages of this gradual process are similar to the social maturation of the child, who passes from the one-to-one relationship with his mother, to his *rapport* with the immediate family, then with the school and finally larger groups.

Music therapy offers simple means to follow the gradual development if needed, with children as well as with adults. An individual may be musically ready to sing or play with others without being psychologically ready to function in a group. The music therapist should first work with him individually, and help him to build through music a one-to-one, mother-child relation-

1 Rudolf Dreikurs, M.D., 'The Impact of Music on Group Therapy and Music Education', *MT* (1959), p. 93.

ship, until he is ready to join a very small listening or music-making group. This technique is used with success at the Menninger Foundation where the gradual passage from individual to group therapy is prescribed by the doctor. The process is made possible by the fact that this hospital runs on purpose a number of therapeutic music groups of different sizes from duets to a full orchestra of twenty or more people. For instance, a patient scheduled by his doctor first for individual clarinet lessons can be moved when prescribed to a small woodwind ensemble which is finally integrated in the orchestra.[1]

Individual and Group Therapy

'A boy age 19 had uncontrollable outbursts of hostile, destructive behaviour, boastfulness, and an attitude of contempt for other people's opinions and rights. Coupled with this lack of control of hostility was an intense need to be accepted by the group and a longing for affection and warmth which he had never known. There was no question but that the hostility directed towards both parental and sibling figures prevented just the acceptance he needed so badly. He played a band instrument and it was felt that use could be made of his interest in music to supplement the therapeutic programme which was designed to foster control of the hostility and increase the gratification he could get from interpersonal relationships.

'To this end participation in two aspects of music was prescribed by his physician. One of these consisted of daily sessions at the piano for lessons and practice with a music therapist who was a warm motherly person. With a combination of gentleness and firmness she was able to engage his attention for increasing periods of time. She first chose exercises and selections in which he could pound and bang on the piano, and then gradually modified

[1] Forrest Slaughter, 'A Transition from Individual to Group Therapy', *MT* (1957), pp. 85–90.

these as the need for such outlets diminished. Duets afforded her an opportunity to demonstrate to him the pleasure to be obtained from co-operative efforts.

'When his aggressive behaviour was sufficiently under control to permit more activity with groups, he became a member of the patients' dance band. This was an activity he was interested in, yet soon he discovered that his behaviour was so disruptive to the group that he could not continue as a member unless he was able to modify it. Helpful suggestions from the therapist and opportunities for leadership in those areas where his skills permitted it, helped him to overcome the initial difficulties. Then he found that the other patients in the band became more genuinely friendly and even admired his musical ability. The relationship between control of hostility, gratification in personal contacts and praise for real achievement was clearer from the experience itself than words alone could ever convey.'[1]

There are many ways of using this one-to-one relationship technique leading to group relationship with musical means, even as simple as a single sound. We have recently watched a woman music therapist using primitive speaking African drums with a group of schizophrenic patients unable to communicate together. The varied pitch of these drums and their different tone colour are striking; they seem to express different voices or personalities. The therapist began with a one-to-one relationship, one patient echoing on his drum the sound she had made on hers. Little by little the activity developed into a kind of series of non-verbal questions and answers from one drum to the other. At that stage other patients were drawn in one after the other. Each with his own drum and his own personal sound[2]

---

[1] Ruth I. Barnard, PH.D., M.D., Senior Psychiatrist, Menninger Foundation, *Journal of the American Medical Women's Association*, Vol. 8, No. 8, August 1953, pp. 266–8.
[2] See p. 16.

became part of the whole without losing his identity. The group was formed at a non-verbal level of integration similar to the 'nature concerts' already described.[1]

The questions and answers on drums are a purely non-verbal form of communication, but they can become quite complex on account of the individuality of the tone of each instrument and the extreme variety of rhythms possible on them; they may come very near a verbal expression. Carl Orff and others use the rhythmical and individual quality of the spoken voice to do ensemble work in which the individual is conscious of the group.

Such techniques are easy to apply at a simple level. They give good results with patients unable to learn a specific technique or with short-term patients who should integrate with a group rapidly and safely. They are also successful with patients whose mind is at primitive level, or not reachable with sophisticated means, such as the mentally retarded or the autistic psychotic patient.

Except in such cases, the musical contribution of the patient to the group should be musically as good as possible, since he must be musically acceptable to a group aiming at some musical result. The music therapist should assess his musical ability and proceed accordingly with the group in mind. A patient with no sense of rhythm but a good ear does better on a non-percussive instrument. Similarly a patient possessing no sense of pitch but a good rhythmical response should play a percussion instrument.

When a patient joins a music group in which he becomes socially and emotionally involved, the activity ceases to be recreational. The group creates allegiances, and even if it is run on a very permissive basis it demands from each of its members acceptable music behaviour.

All therapists in charge of a music group agree that it can help to fulfil a number of social needs within the group: it can

[1] See p. 16.

give an opportunity for choice and freedom of expression; liberate certain energies; help to correct or to foster certain attitudes. The music group is a protected situation out of which leaders can emerge, take responsibility, and may be allowed to make decisions for themselves or for the group. This last factor is important, since some patients suffer from indecision and often wait for others to take responsibility on their behalf. Especially when they are hospitalised, decisions are made for them on almost all matters. The protection they are given may make more threatening a return to responsibility after discharge.

In a music session some decisions have to be taken, choices have to be made, since no group can function unless it is organised and has direction, even at the most elementary practical level: for instance, the seats or the stands for the orchestra must be placed in the right position, someone has to look after the music for the choir. In a music-making group each member has a part to play and is responsible for it. The music therapist must, as unobtrusively as possible, encourage the participation of each member of the group according to their musical and social ability. At some hospitals or special schools the patients give concerts to an invited audience. Then the group can assert even better its personality, and often behaves exactly as a music group of normal amateurs would do in a similar situation, exhibiting stage fright, gratification, anxiety, the pleasure of being in the limelight, and living an exciting situation in which the real and the imaginary may not be distinguishable from each other.

We find in any therapeutic group a number of people whose behaviour is unpredictable or even objectionable, whose musical ability may be low. But since they all belong to the group, social and musical tolerance is the key to their interpersonal relationship, the kind of tolerance which comes from a mutual acceptance of self and others. Musical good behaviour, namely the respect of musical rules, reflects much of the patient's attitude towards himself and others. His attitude may also reveal unfulfilled needs of which perhaps he is not even conscious. The withdrawn, the regressed, the perfectionist, the bully or the egocentric react in different ways to a group situation. Although the music group is in essence a permissive one aiming at enjoyment, it will resist any undesirable behaviour that would spoil its function; it will not tolerate disrupting elements and may even fight against them.

The musical result is bound to the social behaviour and the attitude towards music of the individual, which reflect each other. Regular voluntary attendance to the music session, obedience to the conductor's beat or singing in time are different but indivisible ties that hold the group together. Both may require an effort of will from the patient. Time on the clock and time in music are two realities to which every member has to conform.

In the singing or playing group each member is assigned a specific musical part and a physical place among others. Physical closeness creates between the members a certain relationship even if they do not communicate verbally. Moreover, each of them produces musical sounds that make his presence felt by the others. Each individual becomes a musical entity and as such may be pleasant or objectionable to the members. A wrong note or a beautiful sound heard at proximity makes the player or the singer become real to his neighbour.

The purely musical relationship between the parts influences human relationship. A player or a singer can be solely responsible for an individual part or share it with others.

The relative importance of his part within the group affects each of the members. Madrigal singing or mass singing produces a very different effect on the singer. Sharing a musical part may involve reading from the same sheet, using the same music

stand, turning over for a partner, in short it requires the co-
operation of two individuals within the group. The leader of the
group may have a privileged position, but his behaviour towards
the group has to be acceptable.

Those and many others are the factors which help the music
therapist to integrate the various human and musical elements he
has to blend in a group. A small group can be conducted on a
permissive basis, but a larger one demands the discipline necessary to hold the patients together; thus its effect on the individual is less marked.

The motivation to belong to a music group is mostly emotional. Music therapists try to make their groups attractive to
different kinds of patients. Most of them wish to join for the sake
of the music itself, which gives them enjoyment and emotional
release. The nature and degree of their satisfaction depends on
the way the session is conducted.

We find other patients who join the music group for social
reasons, in order to belong, to have something to do, or just out
of boredom. Whatever their motivation an experienced music
therapist can help most of them to benefit from the group. The
difficulty may be a technical one namely to find a part for each
of the members. It may also happen that the least able or gifted
ones are those who wish to be in the limelight and to do solo
work, or that the gifted and skilful ones refuse to take an important part. It is interesting to observe that quite often the group
itself reacts in the way beneficial to its existence.

Whether in a hospital, a club or a special school, the music
group is part of a larger entity. We have observed in a number of
places that the music group has a certain influence on the whole
community, perhaps because it is based on live sound, not coming
out of a machine, and because it creates an impression of actual
enjoyment shared by a number of people.

In turn the attitude of the community towards the music

group is instrumental in the success or the failure of the group and may increase or undermine its therapeutic value. The interest or the indifference of the high administrative staff of any institution affects the attitude of the medical, nursing or teaching staff towards the music group, which is in need of their goodwill for its good functioning.

In a number of hospitals some members of the medical or nursing staff take much interest in the music group or even share in their musical activities. In a well-known British orthopaedic hospital the long-term patients who can play reasonably well are invited to join the staff amateur orchestra. We also know that the late Dr Sydney Mitchell used to conduct a band of his mental patients. The co-operation of the ward nurses can be invaluable when the music therapist is in need of assistance. In some hospitals he trains in the work those who are musically able and volunteer to help. They can conduct simple sessions of recreational music which enable the patients to enjoy music more frequently. The relationships thus created in the wards themselves are invaluable.

The integrating power of music is specially valuable in psychiatric social clubs, where the integration of the whole organisation depends on the strength of each of the groups it contains. We have often noticed that in a number of these social clubs a well-integrated music group, however small, can be a strong uniting force within the whole body, irrespective of the number of members taking part in its activities. This small group belongs to the whole; it brings a feeling of live, human enjoyment to the club. Most of the members of the club consider it as an asset to the organisation. Moreover, the music group can contribute to many of the other activities of the club.[1]

[1] Juliette Alvin, 'Music in a Psychiatric Social Club', The Aryan Path, January 1960.

The Listening Group

In a group of patients listening to music—not just hearing it played in the background—we can observe reactions similar to those of the playing group, provided that they can be fairly attentive. Each of the members shares a common experience, although his inner interpretation of the music is purely subjective. The group should not be too large to stay intimate and to allow for interpersonal relationship, but large enough to provoke group contagion. Our experience is that a group of ten to twenty-five listeners is in most cases reasonable for a therapeutic approach.

The mood of a group is a definite phenomenon. All teachers know that every day they are facing a class whose general mood is influenced by imponderable factors. The similar phenomenon occurs in any group of patients and is often more marked than with normal people. The mood of the group is immediately felt or sensed by anyone sensitive to such influences. A music therapist facing his group may communicate with them more quickly if she begins by improvising at the piano something spontaneous which reflects the mood of the group instead of playing a set piece. Moreover, unfamiliar pieces are known to provoke deeper reactions than familiar ones.

The aim of music sessions during which live music is played by the music therapist, or if live music is not possible, on records, is to integrate each member of the group and to build up a collective memory of feelings and facts which binds the members together; to create interpersonal relationships based on a common emotional experience; to focus general attention on a number of combined visual and auditory perceptions.

Music can arouse collective feelings such as curiosity, pleasure, satisfaction, emotional release or enthusiasm. Even a meaningful silence between the items, or a long pause in the music, is a strong non-verbal means of uniting the group and can be very successful if well handled, since it works on a common feeling of expectation. We can observe certain reactions spread among the group, sometimes amounting to real communion of feelings. Certain reactions could not happen outside the group, as in the following cases which we have already quoted elsewhere:

'We were invited to give a concert in a psychiatric residential home for adolescent boys, all very disturbed, aggressive, intelligent delinquents, the type who associates freely only towards destructive ends.

'We offered to three different groups of fifteen to twenty boys each, a programme of live music on the cello. Twenty was the maximum possible, and there was great danger of finding in each group leaders who would disrupt.

'We did not ask for discipline—only interest, which was intense from the beginning during an experience which was to the boys totally new and unexpected. We treated them as any other intelligent and sensitive audience whom we respected and with whom we shared our pleasure in music. Each face in the audience was marked with deep trouble and looked as if nothing good or happy could ever happen. The boys relaxed when they found an experience that could be stimulating without tension, and in a world in which it was easy not to revolt. The programme was made to appeal to their intelligence and their imagination and enabled them to display some knowledge. We were able to handle them with a sense of humour—something quite rare with boys who are suspicious and ready to take offence. From beginning to end each of the groups showed attention, interest and enthusiasm.

'A few days after the performance a number of boys asked the psychiatrist in charge if they could form a music club in the home. This very unexpected request was a proof that the musical experience had answered an emotional need, and that a music group could help them towards creative and constructive activities.'[1]

In this case—and we could quote many others—the music therapist did not assume the role of a psychotherapist. This was quite outside her field. But she provided the material on which the psychiatrist could work and which might not have been obtainable easily outside a music group. She then followed and helped the progress made by the patients under psychotherapy.

In similar cases, the closest collaboration between the two therapists is indispensable.

Group Psychotherapy

Provided that such collaboration exists, a music group is a rewarding situation for group psychotherapy. Music can easily provoke verbalisation, sometimes simply as an instinctive response to sound. We can observe this in waiting-rooms and other places provided with background music. But some experiments have shown that if stimulating background music increased the verbalisation of a group of patients, relaxing music had the opposite effect.[2]

At a more conscious level, music can be a projective means. It creates an emotional state in which the patient is ready to reveal his problems, his obsessions and his inhibitions and to face them within the group. The patient may try to describe freely the emotions, sensations or images that the music has evoked in him which are, as in all listeners, related to his past experiences. Moreover, the discussion on the music itself can include the composer as a man, his personality, his emotional

---

[1] Juliette Alvin, *Music for the Handicapped Child*, p. 100.
[2] Leo Shatin and Carl Zimet, 'Influence of Music upon Verbal Participation in Group Psychotherapy', *Diseases of the Nervous System*, 19–66–72, February 1958, quoted in *Journal of Music Therapy*, June 1964, p. 43.

or sexual life and the problems he had to face. Thus music and its many facets may help to release suppressed material which is then openly discussed and interpreted by the psychotherapist.

The Greeks, in a simple form, had already discovered what the late Dr Sydney Mitchell stated in 1948, that music can be a form of group psychotherapy. He strongly and wisely differentiated between the recreational and therapeutic use of music and made valuable experiments in what he called 'specific music therapy'. At Warlingham Park Hospital he made his patients listen to sessions of live music followed by a discussion. He has described some of his experiments, unfortunately not pursued on account of his untimely death.

'One group consisted of approximately equal numbers of manic depressives and schizophrenics with a few neurotics and psychopaths. Patients were of both sexes and consisted of young and middle-aged adults. . . . The average attendance at any session has been about a dozen. It has been found better to restrict the numbers to this maximum in order to improve free conversation and the harmony of the group. Sessions have been held for one hour once a week with occasional extra meetings.

'We wished to observe how far the emotions aroused could be experienced in common both positively and negatively. We encouraged self-expression, self-understanding and improvement of interpersonal, including doctor-patient, relationships. These aims were fostered by discussion and also, at times, by interpretation *to* the patients of their own emotional reactions.'[1]

Dr Mitchell used live music, other psychiatrists prefer recorded music for practical purposes, and also because it may then be a permanent factor in research on the subject. But Dr Donald Blair warns us that 'the manner in which the music is presented

[1] Dr Sydney D. Mitchell, M.A., M.B., D.P.M., from *The Hospital*, October 1948.

to the patient is of the utmost consequence and it is here that the experience of the music therapist is needed.'[1]

A number of psychiatrists have studied the effect made on the group by different types of music. Mitchell observed that what he calls 'serious contemporary music', probably less familiar than the classical or the popular, helped inhibited patients to bring repressed emotions into consciousness. This observation is somewhat confirmed by Newman, who says that 'unfamiliar music is of greater value for stimulating imagery and projection'.[2] Mitchell found that romantic music does not help group integration, since it arouses personal association and creates tension. But Newman, treating his group on Freudian lines, has observed that if tension is aroused by repressed material coming to the surface 'subsequent interpretation and adjustment lead to the dissolution of conflict and relief of tension'.[3] Mitchell, who experimented on more varied types of music, found that classical music seemed to help towards the cohesion of the group because of the sense of security it aroused. But traditional music and folk songs were by far 'the most effective way to bring people together and to integrate the group because of their deep-seated and cosmic relationship'.[4]

We may at the end of this chapter mention a modern experiment with music during the sleeping cure of mental patients. The treatment bears striking similarity to the ancient group sleeping cures at Epidaurus, where the patients slept together in a large room and dreams were part of the cure, subsequently interpreted by the priest. Unfortunately for us, although it is

[1] Donald Blair, M.D., D.P.M., 'Music Therapy', *New Society*, 30 January 1964.
[2] Dr Newman, *Symposium on Music Therapy, Tension and Relaxation*, pub. by Society for Music Therapy and Remedial Music (1964), p. 3.
[3] Ibid., p. 3.
[4] Dr Sydney D. Mitchell, M.A., M.B., D.P.M., 'Music in Mental Hospitals', *The Hospital*, October 1948, reprint.

likely to have occurred, we do not know if music and incantations went on once the patients were asleep.

The experiment made in 1958 in the French psychiatric hospital at Bonneval was on the effect of music on the collective cure method with seven patients sleeping in the same room. The group situation was supposed to be essential to the treatment and to be favourable to the occurrence of dreams which might not have happened otherwise.

Specially recorded music was played before and during the sleep. It was found that musical stimulation had some influence on the occurrence of dreams. They revealed certain states of anxiety, euphory, erotism, guilt, fear and others, seemingly related to the character of the music and were given psychological interpretation.

We do not know whether the group situation influenced the individual reaction to the experience. These reactions will be discussed with others of a similar kind in the next chapter.

The Individual

The music group is formed of individuals whose reactions we observe and assess. The reaction of the group is an aggregate of individual responses. Ultimately these are the most important. They have to be observed separately and assessed in consequence. It may not be possible or beneficial to the patient to include him in a music group. Sometimes it would not be good even for him to have music therapy in any form.

A number of psychiatrists who recognise the general value of music therapy agree that its application is not always advisable with patients who have a musical past. The beneficial effect of music sometimes depends on the place that music has occupied in the patient's life, of its association, which it may be desirable either to re-awaken or to leave dormant. It is not always desirable that he should hear music reminding him of certain circumstances, or to play again on his instrument. We have occasionally met such patients. For instance, a manic depressive, who had played before his illness was shown a violin. He would not touch it, although he seemed tempted to do so. After a few days he mentioned that his playing the violin has been 'the source of all the trouble with his father'. Another patient, a good pianist, had developed an acute state of anxiety which resulted in such muscular tension that he could scarcely play, although he tried to force himself and thus made things even worse. He was deeply frustrated, since he missed the emotional release he had in the past received from playing music. At that stage and in his state it might have been disastrous to put him in a music group, and probably premature for him to have individual music therapy, unless the individual therapy could have been complementary to the psychiatric treatment. We cannot always assume that because the patient has done it before his illness it is good for him to play, sing or listen to music.

In fact, some patients find it unbearable to have contact with music. Sommer tells of a schizophrenic patient who could not bring herself to play the piano, because the piano was not hers and music was too full of associations anyway.[1] She also, in the same paper, tells of a depressive patient who found music too painful during his illness and made every effort to avoid it. Drs Zanker and Glatt studied the conscious response of certain mental patients to music. One of them expressed the same feelings, that music revived memories of fallen hopes and lost ideals and made him feel that life was too hard.

They also observed some violent responses in aggressive patients. A hostile psychopath confessed that listening to music made him feel uncontrollable and violent and angry with his

---

[1] Jane Hillyer, *Reluctantly Told*, MacMillan, New York (1931), quoted by Dorothy T. Sommer, *Music in the Autobiography of Mental Patients*, unpublished paper (1960).

fellow men. Another stated that 'when he listened to music in a group he found that other people's attitudes seemed to interfere with his and this made him irritable'.[1]

Adverse reactions to music as well as favourable ones may provide a clue useful to the psychiatric treatment. Many reactions are due not to the music itself and bear no resemblance to it, but to the personality of the patient, to his illness, or to past memories.

Normal and sick people usually react to music in the same way, but a sane reaction may become pathological in its consequences. What is important is to extract from the response what may be of therapeutic value.

We presume, on the whole, that patients hear music normally, but their interpretation of sound may be pathological. Mental illness may produce a certain attitude to sound itself. Lupo and Hercher have made a specific study of the subject and suggest that 'certain types of mental illness, particularly schizophrenia, cause the individual to take a very common sound and build a situation around it that demands some defensive position to be taken in relation to it', a concept that may give sound itself a threatening meaning.[2]

They have also observed that a schizophrenic patient seems to have difficulty in locating the physical source of sound. 'When he is hallucinating in the auditory sphere he almost invariably indicates that the sounds are coming from behind or above him but never in front within his visual field.'[3] He feels that the sounds he cannot identify come from a third person—'they' or 'he'—even if he is himself the cause of the sound. This impression

[1] Drs A. Zanker and M. M. Glatt, 'Experiments with Music in a Mental Hospital', *Monthly Review of Psychiatry and Neurology*, 131, No. 4 (1956), pp. 215–25.

[2] Sonic Apperception Test. William E. Hercher, Psychologist, Thomas G. Lupo, M.D., Neuropsychiatrist, *MT* (1952), pp. 268–9.

[3] Ibid.

may produce in him a feeling of fear and anxiety and can apply to music.

We cannot assume, in spite of the usual belief in the benevolence of music, that sound or music is not to certain patients a threatening experience. The matter is controversial. Dr Rudolf Dreikurs[1] assumes that 'music eliminates the primitive fear of unorganised sounds' which we have discussed in the first chapter, and Ruppenthal[2] has observed that even the paranoid whose illness is to distort all logic does not distort music as a threat.

Sommer suggests that the psychotic may perceive music differently from the normal. The remark made by Esquirol that his patients found the tones false may support her opinion, which was tested on normal subjects who took voluntarily hallucinatory drugs—LSD or others—and who reported striking changes in auditory perception, especially with regard to music. When they were under the drugs they found that some rhythmical music seemed to be overwhelming or frightening, and ordinary popular pieces felt absurd and ridiculous.[3]

The psychiatrists, Zanker and Glatt, have compared the so-called normal or rational responses to music to the responses to the same pieces of their neurotic or psychopath patients. Both have been struck by the relative frequency of the patients' incongruous responses, an incongruity not justified by indifference or ignorance; some of the patients were musically well educated.

Their responses seemed to be a mirror of their actual mood, not at all related to the character of the music which was obvious. A neurotic found gay and light music sorrowful, black or restless; a male psychopath projected his own facade of defence, optimism

[1] Rudolf Dreikurs, M.D., 'The Dynamics of Music Therapy', *MT* (1953), p. 16.

[2] Wayne W. Ruppenthal, 'Experimental Determinants of Perception, Some Considerations for Music Therapy', *MT* (1954), pp. 53–60.

[3] Dorothy T. Sommer, *Music in the Biography of Mental Patients*, Unpublished paper (1960).

and cheerfulness that covered his selfishness and unreliability and found the music gleeful, joyful or uplifting whatever was played.

The physicians state that 'these incongruous responses often proved of some diagnostic value by throwing some light on the personalities of the patients, on their unconscious attitudes and conflicts, and thus indirectly were of value to psychotherapy'.[1] They also observed that in several cases, when the patients improved in a general way, the incongruity of their responses to music gradually disappeared.

The patient who hears music in a normal way may, just because it is normal, erect a defence mechanism in order not to be reached. A woman patient has described in detail the development of her emotional contacts with the music towards a deep and healing experience. She was musically responsive and knew that music had to be therapeutically used.

Although she found at first that the listening session was the only time when she could rest from her inner turmoil, she acknowledged resisting for weeks being emotionally reached. Gradually she felt more and more free within herself to choose in the music different types of emotional experiences. First she responded to its regularity and control. Then she began to share in its expression of warmth, joy, beauty or sorrow as she chose, but in an impersonal way not related to any human being. She also felt that the continuous movement within the music could help her to fight against her own inner restlessness.

In the following stage she began to relate to the composers who, she felt, must have experienced feelings similar to hers. She could trust them and communicate with them as fellow human beings. Music then seemed to evoke in her feelings of kindness, hope and acceptance of herself. She believed that this stage was the turning-point in her general treatment and she

[1] A. Zanker and M. M. Glatt, op. cit.

began to relate to other people. It was the most important part of her recovery.[1]

This experience is exceptionally interesting, because the results were due to the patient's consciousness of an emotional process that she was able to control herself during the 'listening hours'. She was obviously an extremely musically sensitive person, but nothing she says in her long text indicates that she was musically educated. She quotes no composer and no style of music. Her concentration and power of attention were good enough for her to be conscious of the developments taking place and of their relations to the music.

The breaking up of defences is one of the most generally accepted effects of music in psychotherapy. Music can become a bridge between reality and the unreal world in which the patient is isolated or takes refuge.

In breaking up the defences, music can help to uncover unconscious attitudes or to bring out to the surface memories or feelings hidden in the subconscious. This process does not necessarily require cathartic music. Making or listening to music can in a gentle way mollify or penetrate what has been called the secret recesses of the soul. Contrary to the effect of strongly structured classical music, Dr Sydney Mitchell has observed that impressionist music, that is music of a sensuous, fluid character, enables the listener to drift along with the music and gives greater opportunities for deep-seated ideas to come to the surface.[2]

We have observed that it often is the dreamy, non-emotional, sensuous quality of music that penetrates without provoking the patient's resistance to more potent music. Moreover, sensuous melodic music has a physically relaxing effect and helps towards

[1] Quoted by Wayne W. Ruppenthal, op. cit., *MT* (1954), pp. 53–58.
[2] Dr Sydney Mitchell, M.D., D.P.M., 'Music and Psychological Medicine', *Proceedings of the Royal Musical Association*, Session L XXVII.

relaxation. It makes no emotional or dynamic demands on the listener.

Music is a non-verbal aesthetic experience, it carries no moral implications that could create resistance, and no sense of sin which words may suggest. Nevertheless, its association can evoke unhealthy, ugly memories of jealousy, frustration or humiliation that must be handled with great understanding by the therapist. This happened in the case of the child whose father was in prison. Martin, a deeply maladjusted boy, hospitalised in a home for emotionally disturbed children, was in revolt against the world, and unable to open up. One evening before going to sleep he heard more or less consciously a recorded performance of Vaughan Williams's tragic and desolate 'Sinfonia Antarctica'. When he woke up he gave up all resistance and began to sob, saying that the music had reminded him of his father in prison for another eight years. All his sorrow and humiliation came to the surface and could then be dealt with by the therapist. At last he was helped to come to terms with life and regained his inner peace.[1]

Most psychiatrists and physicians are quite outspoken about the psychological knowledge and the musical skill that a music therapist should possess. He is handling a powerful tool and cannot any more work on trial and error. This time has passed. Moreover, his work must be complementary to the treatment and he has to understand the causes and the nature of the illness.

Individual music-therapy sessions demand the utmost of what a music therapist can offer.

In a music group, the patient feels in some way protected by the group; he can be more or less anonymous and feels less exposed. Musically, he can be taken at his own standard so long as he behaves in a socially acceptable manner. In individual

[1] J. Alvin, *Music for the Handicapped Child*, pp. 97–98 (from F. Knight).

sessions, even the most permissive music therapist makes demands on the patient who is meant to play, to learn or to listen to music. In the process the therapist helps him to evaluate himself, to increase his self-knowledge and to adopt a more healthy attitude towards his problems. The patient often meets in music certain problems related to his personal difficulties, that the music therapist can exploit successfully according to the medical instructions. A British music therapist has expressed her opinion in a paper full of wisdom and experience: 'With patients sent for individual treatment it is necessary to be given clear instructions by the psychiatrist about what he hopes to achieve. Subsequently any emotional reactions or information which may come up during the music session will be evaluated and used by him. It hardly needs stressing that this rather specialised and difficult kind of treatment is quite without value unless the physician and the musician work in the closest touch.'[1]

For instance, we may discover in certain patients an 'innate musical personality' which they can express in primitive sounds and which often reflects their actual state or reveals some characteristics of their disorder. Among a number of responses to music of psychotic children, Nordoff and Robbins have analysed and classified at least eight types of rhythmical beating of drums and cymbals, namely the disorderly, the compulsive, the evasive and so on. Such observations can help towards the diagnosis of the psychotic state of the patient and enable the physician to follow up developments which may occur during the course of the psychological treatment.[2]

The one-to-one relationship in individual music therapy is

[1] Mair Brooking, A.R.C.M., 'Music in the Treatment of Mental Illness', *Mental Health*, Vol. XVII, No. 1, Autumn 1957, pp. 4–9.

[2] Paul Nordoff and Clive Robbins, *Music Therapy for Handicapped Children*, Rudolf Steiner publication Inc., 151 North Moison Road, Blauvelet, New York (1965), pp. 52–64.

fraught with dangers, especially with possessive, jealous and demanding patients whose relationship with the music therapist may become very emotional. In an analytical situation, the fact that music adds a third person may be disturbing unless a perfect harmony exists in the teamwork of the physician and the musician. Again and again, in speaking or in writing, physicians have repeated and emphasised what Pargeter had already stated in the eighteenth century.[1]

We may quote Dr Joel of the U.S.A., who states that the aims of music therapy must be understood in order to meet the needs of the patient: 'Attitudes to promote greater integration of the personality must be thoroughly understood by the therapist and an overall treatment plan kept clearly in mind. This treatment or therapy situation is not an easy one and calls for a great deal of ingenuity, self-discipline and maturity on the part of the therapist to best help the patient.'[2]

Music therapy is usually a long-term process which can be understood only by following every step of the treatment. We have selected three examples in which the development took place through gradual stages:

INDIVIDUAL THERAPY

Case I

A young woman, twenty-three years old, impulsive, demanding, aggressive, pushed people's patience to the limit and constantly provoked rejection. Hurt feelings and sulky behaviour would follow with no awareness that she had done anything to disturb, annoy or provoke the other person. Consequently everyone was viewed as hostile, an enemy, and the cycle was started again.

[1] pp. 55–78.
[2] Dr Charles Joel, M.D., 'New Developments in Psychiatry and their Relation to Music Therapy', *Bulletin of N.A.M.T.*, Vol. VI, No. 2, May 1957.

This had been going on all her life and could be seen in its greatest intensity in relation to her mother, who rejected her.

Our first therapeutic goal was to increase her awareness of the ways in which she contributed to her own unhappiness, of how her behaviour affected other people, of how she provoked rejection and then reacted to it with more hostility. Only after this goal was reached did we feel we could begin to help her understand the reasons behind her behaviour and how she might change it to more satisfying ends. It was hoped that her interest in music could be used in achieving these goals.

Piano lessons were prescribed, not to increase her musical knowledge or ability, but to use her relationship with the music therapist to call her attention to the various facets of her behaviour as they appeared during the lesson. In the course of treatment there was ample opportunity for this. The therapist's patience was tried again and again, the same simple mistakes were made repeatedly, pointed out to her, corrected, made again, then blamed on the therapist. She insisted on skipping necessary preliminaries and plunging into music far beyond her ability. If denied, she felt absurd and deprived; if permitted to court failure in this way, she was not sufficiently protected. The hours for teaching and practice time were either inconvenient or insufficient. Within the music-therapy situation, one character trait and behaviour pattern after another appeared. Through it all the therapist's attention was directed to the patient, not to the music, and she dealt with things on the spot as they happened. Why these all appeared in such concentrated form in relation to the music lessons it was difficult to say, but its value was obvious. Instead of many people dealing piecemeal with the problems in a variety of situations, it was possible to concentrate the confrontations and suggestions in one person and one situation with all others adjunctive to it. One might even say the psychiatrist was an adjunctive therapist in this case.[1]

Case II

This case was reported by a team of two psychiatrists and a music therapist working in a British mental hospital (St Bernard's).

Mrs X, a patient suffering from a neurotic anxiety depression. Disturbed relationships in early childhood and present marital difficulties gave rise to severe conflicts and her realisation that she would never bear children and led to an acute breakdown.

In this case the value of music therapy was very marked. The psychotherapeutic sessions centred in emotions and memories awakened by the music and the patient's resistance was quickly broken down. She improved steadily and found deep satisfaction in her own music-playing. She is now well and working.[2]

Case III

In the following case the music therapist was called in because the patient's inability to communicate made psychological treatment very difficult. Music was treated as a means of non-verbal communication at first, the music being impersonal, played on records and not by the therapist. The music session was meant as a conditioning to the psychological treatment immediately following.

Some patients who have some difficulty in responding to psychotherapy because of marked depression or extreme anxiety receive a thirty-minute music session immediately preceding the

[1] Ruth I. Barnard, PH.D., M.D., Senior Psychiatrist, Menninger Foundation, *Journal of the American Medical Women's Association*, Vol. 8, No. 8, August 1953, pp. 266-8.

[2] Donald Blair, M.D., D.P.M., T. A. Werner, M.D., D.P.M., and M. Brooking, 'The Value of Individual Music Therapy as an Aid to Individual Psychotherapy', *International Journal of Social Psychiatry*, Vol. VII, No. 1, 1961, pp. 54-64.

hour of psychotherapy, the technique being adapted to the individual needs of the patient. A patient was diagnosed as having a depressive reaction. She was suicidal and she had a poverty of interpersonal contacts. Her difficulty in relating socially stemmed from her belief that she had nothing of value to offer to anyone in a social situation. She was referred by the psychologist because of intense anxiety and her inability to spontaneous communication during psychotherapy. During the patient's first three music-therapy sessions semi-classical records were played. The music therapist made no attempt to communicate verbally on an interpersonal basis with the patient. An occasional comment on the beauty of the music and the relaxing effect it produced on the therapist was interjected by the therapist at appropriate times. Records played in the fourth session were those chosen by the patient and the ability of the music to soothe and relax the listener was maintained with the conversational topics broadening to other impersonal areas. At the following session the patient expressed a desire to learn to play the piano. Lessons were begun. The psychologist reported positive results on an *a priori* basis.[1]

So far, we have described individual music therapy as a slow, gradual process. But it is not and has not always been so. Indeed, in the ancient world most references are to the immediate cathartic effect of music, what Aristotle called a purge of the emotions. 'When he spoke in that way', says Sir David Ross, 'he probably meant the removal of excessive passions, what the psycho-analysts of today call ab-reaction.'[2]

The working off of strong emotions through music can be observed with many patients where pent-up feelings need discharge, in children as in adults. One of our patients, a disturbed

[1] Joy Conrad, *Bulletin of N.A.M.T.*, Vol. XI, No. 3, September 1962, pp. 7–12.
[2] Sir David Ross, *Aristotle*, Methuen & Co. Ltd, London, pp. 283–4.

and agitated woman, used from time to time to come up abruptly to the piano, sit down without a word and run her hands on the keyboard from one end to the other, pounding violently what she called the history of her life. It was a series of uncontrolled outbursts that stopped abruptly and probably were a true picture of her disturbed life.

Ab-reaction can take another form when under the influence and the support of music the patient acts out his inner troubles. In a group of extremely disturbed children to whom we were playing music, we observed a very small boy, withdrawn, sulky and tense. We played a cradle song during which the children were rocking an imaginary baby. The boy suddenly made the gesture to strangle the baby and to throw it on the floor. Then he looked round slyly to see if anybody had seen him. It was the first time he had shown these hidden feelings.

When the child or the adult is in need of acting a long and painful story repressed in the subconscious, the immaterial, elusive, non-verbal and continuous sound of music can give support and help the patient to act out the experience to its end. This can be achieved when the therapist improvises in the background music of the suitable mood and speed, and follows the movements of the patient without imposing or suggesting anything through music or speech. The patient may then go through the whole sequence as did a little girl in a centre for severely maladjusted children. The therapist improvised music that gave the child some incentive to move about and a protective feeling. The little girl went round and round muttering to herself, imagining herself in a dark wood in the moonlight looking for some unknown thing. She searched under the leaves, found a baby doll and started eating it. It is doubtful that she would have gone through the experience without the help of the music.[1]

[1] Juliette Alvin, *Music for the Handicapped Child*, O.U.P. (1965), p. 98.

In the last two, as in many other similar cases, suppressed or repressed emotions of an undesirable kind were released through a violent outburst. The psychotherapeutic method of arousing such emotions cannot be used safely without giving the patient some means or the necessary support enabling him to control its effects and to bring it definitely into consciousness. Once the music has produced such effect the psychiatrist should be in charge of its results.

The traumatic effect of a musical experience may produce lasting results. They should not be confused with the effects made by a change of mood which, however rapid, is not likely to last.

The fact that a mood created by music is not lasting should not detract from its usefulness. In medicine some drugs which produce only temporary results are valuable to the treatment, and so is music. It may also provide a breathing-space during which a medical treatment can be applied.

Music can help the patient to react better to medical treatment by putting him in a more receptive mood, relaxing him if he is tense, stimulating him if he is apathetic, making him more aware of his surroundings if he is withdrawn.

Not all music produces the expected mood. Some patients are allergic to certain sounds. To others music recalls experiences that destroy the effect of certain pieces. The musical idiosyncrasies of a patient may be observed, but not explained. For instance, seventeenth-century music usually brings a mood of stability and repose, even when stimulating or emotional. One of our patients' nerves were always set on edge when he heard Elizabethan music. He revealed after some time that it reminded him of a school teacher he had detested and who had a passion for seventeenth-century music. The man could not yet be reconciled with it, or dissociate madrigals from hated memories.

When music is used in close relation to psychotherapy the task of the music therapist is often to induce the right kind of mood, at the right time. The factors involved are varied and variable, but we have seen that music possesses infinite resources and flexibility. Dr Barnard has observed in a number of cases the psychophysiological value of music on the mood and behaviour of some hypo-or hyper-active patients, and how it can help the patient to make better use of other therapies.[1]

Dr Blair and others in Britain express the same opinion, based on their own experience:

'The psychotherapists found that music-therapy sessions immediately prior to psychotherapy sessions facilitated the emergence of repressed unconscious material which was of much psychotherapeutic value. It was worked through forthwith and this seemed in particular to increase the patients' insight. . . .

'In those cases whose interviews did not precede psychotherapy the reports forwarded to the psychotherapists were valuable, but the value of the music-therapy session seemed to be diminished by the interval before psychotherapy took place. . . .

'As far as we can judge patients treated with psychotherapy in combination with music usually responded to treatment more rapidly and required total treatment of a shorter duration than those receiving psychotherapy alone.'[2]

The magic Iso principle is fundamental in the induction of moods, meeting the patient first in his actual emotional climate. This technique works well, even with mentally retarded patients, so long as the experience does not exceed their span of attention and is at their mental level. A specialist in mental retardation has made the same observations as other physicians, that the first step in music therapy is to communicate with the patient, where we find him.

[1] Dr Ruth Barnard, M.D., *Journal of American Women's Associations*, Vol. 8, No. 8, August 1953, pp. 266–8.

[2] *The International Journal of Social Psychiatry*, Vol. 7, No. 1, 1961. The Value of Music Therapy as an Aid to Individual Therapy, op. cit.

'To establish a basic *rapport* between the patient and the music the latter must be chosen to fit his frame and speed of mind. An apathetic regressed person, for instance, would be more readily captured with music that is sad and slow than one which is gay and fast, and conversely restless, distracted patients would be more easily reached by music with a loud fast cheerful tempo. Once the therapist has worked himself into the patient's mood and temporarily has held his attention, a shift of attention to a different tempo or a different mood can gradually be developed by the use of music of a contrasting character.'[1]

The fact that music can be apprehended at low brain level makes it invaluable in cases of mental retardation, from the E.S.N. child to the severely subnormal adult. It can work at a primitive level of understanding and feelings. From the individual, the effect can spread to the group, whose reactions may be totally immature, but genuine and beneficial.

The reactions of the mentally retarded to music are quite similar to those observed in patients of normal intelligence, but since they happen at a much lower level, the techniques and the choice of music have to be carefully adapted.

Mental retardation is not curable, therefore the word 'therapy' may not be applicable here. But certain musical techniques can help this patient to develop what is in him, to increase his power of listening and his retention of sequences of sounds, to develop his sense perception and his manipulative skill, to help him to understand elementary causes and effects. Moreover, music can give the mentally retarded pleasures that he may not find in any other way and means of self-expression at his own mental and emotional level. We have already described elsewhere the remedial methods through which such results can be achieved.[2]

[1] F. E. Kratter, D.P.M., 'Music Therapy for the Mentally Retarded', *Bulletin of N.A.M.T.*, Vol. VII, No. 2, May 1958, pp. 9–11.
[2] Juliette Alvin, *Music for the Handicapped Child*.

Music is used in connection with many types of psychological treatment. The analytical concept of id, ego and superego is not incompatible with music therapy. Indeed, music can be and has been discussed in analytical terms.[1] We can deduce from our study that throughout history music has reflected man's three levels of personality and thus helped towards their integration.

The instinctive forces of sex, aggression and destruction can be aroused by music to an uncontrollable degree. It also arouses sensuous pleasure at low brain level.

On a higher plane man has used his intelligence, used sound and made it in his image, shaping its substance through mental discipline and reason and the acceptance of certain rules and conventions. If music has lost some of its elemental power in the process, it has acquired intellectual logic and the power to express emotions under control. Moreover, music seems to possess an ethical character which can influence the development of a healthy personality.

We have seen that music is bound to certain mathematical concepts. In the antiquity it was related to pure science, and still contains an element of the absolute which can satisfy the mind in search of it. Moreover, musical activities are based on the ethical acceptance of these laws. Thus man can tend towards musical perfection as did Bach, who reached it in his last work the Art of Fugue. To the ordinary man, music can represent ideal perfection in a field where there is no sense of guilt or redemption.

Music is a well-known means of sublimation, at superego level. It can express the undesirable, the forbidden, the unspeakable in an acceptable and beautiful form. Sex instinct, for instance, says Charles Singer, 'can be sublimated in other creative channels and there are many altars besides those of Venus at which young men and women may kindle their essential fires'.[2]

---

[1] André Michel, *Psychanalyse de la Musique*, P.U.F., Paris, 1951.
[2] Charles Singer, M.D., *Short History of Medicine*, p. 295.

From Venus young men and women may turn to Apollo.

The physical and psychological sexual characteristics of music take a special significance in music therapy on Freudian lines. Some musical instruments have a phallic shape, others imitate women's breasts. The technique of most instruments is one of physical intimacy between the player and instrument. A guitar is held on the lap; it is more personal than a piano. Wind instruments are oral; the violin is held just above the breast. The tone of musical instruments, just as the tone of the human voice, seems to possess masculine or feminine characteristics. We have already discussed the sexual nature of music, where we usually find a dominant masculine or feminine character to which the listener or the performer responds according to his own nature. A man who is not virile would prefer music with a feminine dominance and vice versa. The latent homosexuality which exists in most music can also affect player and listener alike.

The relationship between music and dreams, music and unconscious states has been observed throughout history. It is curious that the Freudian school has not paid more attention to this relationship. We all know how sound itself can affect our subconscious thoughts, and we are now seeing the development of techniques meant to use our unconscious power of sound retention during sleep.

Diserens quotes an experiment made in 1915 by Stepanov in which music was played to the sleeping patient in an adjoining room. During moments of wakefulness she reported her dreams through a speaking-tube. Stepanov observed that there was subconscious recognition of the music in her dreams. These were of a non-musical or non-auditory character and showed that the auditory stimuli were transformed into images.

The Bonneval experiment was a unique attempt to assess the value of music in sleeping cures used with mental patients. It was conducted on strict experimental lines by two psychiatrists and a musician experienced in this type of work.

The experiment already mentioned[1] helped to show that music can penetrate the subconscious of the sleeping patient and is favourable to the occurrence of dreams which are the essential basis of the particular treatment. It demonstrated that the music can gradually induce the four phases of the therapy—adaptation, regression, tension and re-harmonisation—through which the patient should pass. The music was chosen to provoke a specific stimulus related to the different phases. It consisted of several orchestral extracts from Bartók (The Pursuit) and Ravel (Nocturne and Spring), mostly of an evocative character.

In more than two-thirds of the patients, the dreams corresponded to the general character of the music, and were classified accordingly as related to (1) pleasant optimistic situations, (2) feelings of anxiety, impossibility or flight, (3) troubling situations, enigmas.

Jung was more likely than Freud to give a symbolic meaning to music in dreams. One of his patients, a woman, has given a description of a dream with music, and we have a report of Jung's discussion on the dream related in the American Jungian publication, *Spring*.[2]

'I was trying to play some music and all the different people of my family tried to interfere. I was on a terrace looking out over the sea when a rich Jew at the next table began to play also. The music that he played was so beautiful that I stopped playing for a minute myself to listen to him.

'Have you any idea of what this dream means? It is very simple. What is music? Of course, it is *feeling*. She is very

---

[1] p. 137.

[2] C. G. Jung, 'The Interpretation of Visions', excerpts from the notes of Mary Foote published by the Analytical Psychology Club of New York Inc., Spring 1960, p. 106.

intellectual and has very inferior feeling, so it is probable that we will encounter most of her feeling in the unconscious. The dream brings out that problem. So playing music means giving play to her feelings, compensating her chiefly intellectual attitude. . . .

'But when she tries to play her feelings, use her own feelings, then it becomes evident that every member of the family is against it—she insists that despite the members of the family she will continue to play her feelings. But there is a rich Jew who plays much better than she and therefore she gives up. Yet how can these feelings develop if she cannot use them? . . . But then something subtle happens: namely the opposition of the family does not kill her, but the fact that somebody plays better music —*that* kills her.'

A few analysts are today making a practical, direct use of music in their treatment. Dr Teirich[1] and his followers have experimented on the effects of musical vibrations on the patient during psychotherapy. The vibrations are transmitted through the couch on which he is lying and affect his neuro-muscular system. We understand that this technique is linked with a special psychological treatment called autogenous, a kind of self-hypnosis induced by the patient himself once he is trained to do it. The music can also be heard by the patient and this probably reinforces the effect produced on the nervous system.

Psychotherapeutic musical techniques combined with suggestion or auto-suggestion are practised in a number of countries. They are mostly used with individual cases of anxiety neurosis, emotional disturbance or depression, not usually with psychotic patients. These techniques are allied to Schultz or Teirich autogenous treatment in which music plays an important part. Some recent medical research has carried further the methods of

---

[1] H. R. Teirich, *On Therapeutics through Music and Vibrations, Gravesaner Blatter* (ed. H. Scherschen), Ars Viva Verlag, Mainz (1959), 13.

relaxation and music, for instance in the work of Dr Jean Guilhot.[1] Complete physical passive relaxation achieved through suggestion can help the patient to dissociate his emotions from his mental activity. In this passive state he may be able to disinvolve himself from his obsessions and anxieties and gradually to come back to the reality of his past and present life. From this state he is made to go through several stages towards a slow rebuilding of his personality.

The process goes through relaxation and disidentification, disinvolvement from tense emotions and mental automatism, towards concentration and new involvements. Music is used during each of these stages, following a similar trend and progression. The psychological treatment includes music sessions during which the patient in a receptive state listens first to music reflecting his actual mood; then to music producing in him a gradual change of mood. It is often recommended that the patient's posture should correspond to the desired effect: for instance, sitting and crouching down—lying flat—or sitting straight. The light in the room should be conducive to a state of inner peace and contemplation.

The music chosen for these treatments has been tested for its effects on various listeners. It is meant to follow up and help the gradual stages in the improvement of the patient. We have observed that certain psychological techniques of relaxation are related to and try to promote the development of spiritual values and attitudes of the patient. Then the effect of the music depends not only on the musical sensitiveness of the patient but also on his ability to respond to spiritual experiences. The experiments made by this school of psychotherapy confirm the observations made by many others, that music therapy is often more effective with the musically undiscriminating than

[1] Dr J. et M. A. Guilhot, J. Jost, *Musique, Psychologie et Psychotherapie*, Les Editions Sociales Françaises, Paris (1964).

with the sophisticated listener. In general it has been found that the musically average individual fares best in music therapy.

A number of experiments described in this chapter and linked with psychotherapy aim at the verbalisation of the patient who is helped to uncover his inner feelings, a process which depends on his intelligence and his co-operation. Some other techniques can help him to make a bridge between the unconscious and reality without the use of words. Art and music therapy can combine together, and the patient's artistic performance can be interpreted on the same principles.

Scattered but interesting experiments have been conducted on the effect of background music on paintings or drawings made by mental patients. Some of their work seemed to have been influenced by the unconscious evocative power of music which created or emphasised certain moods in them, as had happened at Bonneval Hospital during unconscious states and were then expressed through the imagery of dreams. Some paintings made to background music of an aggressive primitive character showed abrupt, angular lines, scenes of conflict or flight. Others reflected the colourful or sensuous mood of impressionist music played at the time they were painting.

These experiments may be useful to the diagnosis of an illness or to the assessment of an actual mood. It would be worth while to follow them up, provided that certain factors are available, namely the state of the patient at the time and his innate or acquired receptivity to music which works even when music is not a conscious experience. A patient who listens consciously to music often speaks of his reaction to it, as we have seen in the work of Glatt, Zanker, Mitchell and many others. But instead of using words a patient not verbally inclined may express himself through art, transfer on his painting unspoken feelings aroused by the music and give them pictorial reality. This remark does not apply solely to mental patients; the same process can help the cripple. Some pictures made by physically maimed people after a concert often contain a vivid impression of physical movement which is the kinaesthetic image of an experience of which they are deprived in real life.

V

Present and Future Trends

WE have seen that music used empirically or rationally in magical, religious or scientific healing was not and is not meant to be a cure in itself. The therapeutic value of music resides in the unique help it can offer various medical and remedial treatments. Its modern application requires the rational blending of certain medical and musical disciplines.

The nature of sound and the psychology of music have never changed, nor have the basic physical and psychological characteristics of man. But within a few decades a number of medical treatments have undergone a drastic transformation. The growth of specialised research, the invention of scientific apparatus to detect, or fight against, all kinds of diseases, as well as recent discoveries in biochemistry, have completely transformed the methods of diagnosis and treatment of certain physical and mental illnesses. Such facts may put into question the usefulness of music therapy in the contemporary scene.

In the long term we believe that the advance of medical knowledge has not diminished the value of music therapy in the treatment of illness. Ultimately the patient's recovery depends on how much he can draw on his own physical, mental and emotional resources, which are affected by music in a more or less degree. We have seen that the effects of music have been used through the centuries in relation to all kinds of disorders. The task of the modern music therapist is to apply music to the actual treatment, under medical advice or guidance, and as a member of the therapeutic team.

The Promotion of Music Therapy

The recognition of the music therapist as a member of the team in a medical or rehabilitating situation is vital to the very existence, to the success or failure of music therapy. To our knowledge, there exist only three organisations aiming at the promotion of music therapy: in Great Britain, the Society for Music Therapy and Remedial Music was founded in 1958 by the author of this book; in the United States of America, the National Association for Music Therapy is an older organisation which has functioned since 1950; in South America the Asociación Argentina de Musicoterapia founded in 1966.

The philosophy of these organisations and the techniques they use reflect a national attitude towards music and medicine. But whatever their approach each of them is concerned with the study and the application of music therapy.

The three organisations publish regularly reviews, bulletins, books and various papers. They organise regular meetings and conferences at national and regional level.

The British society has become an important centre of study and information on all aspects of music therapy. It has a number of members in foreign countries. One of its functions is to pool the available information from many parts of the world, to act as consultant or adviser on the many matters concerning the therapeutic use of music.

The American organisation is more of a professional body. For several years it has offered a recognised diploma in music therapy at university level (R.M.T.). In Great Britain a recent post-graduate Course is now awaiting official recognition leading to a diploma in music therapy. On the Continent the Vienna Academy of Music offers a course on the subject, but there is not yet in Austria or elsewhere an organisation similar to those in Britain, America or Argentina.

The Training of Music Therapists

Training is of utmost importance. It is generally accepted that the music therapist should first be a fully trained and experienced musician as were David and Farinelli, but able to apply the psychology of music to his work. Professionally he should be a good performer and improviser, conversant with all types of music, able to undertake a number of tasks such as conducting vocal or instrumental ensembles or giving vocal or instrumental tuition. He must also possess the basic physiological and psychological knowledge indispensable for him to understand the contribution his music can make to the work of his colleagues in the therapeutic team and to carry it through.

But none of this extensive knowledge and skill can be of any value unless the music therapist possesses the right personality. We have discussed the personality of the healer-musician and the importance of the interpersonal relationship between him and the sick man which always affects the treatment. The personal qualities needed to succeed in the field are numerous, some are essential. They include a stable, mature personality, the ability to communicate, to share and to observe, to show warm sympathy and understanding without becoming emotionally involved, to have a sense of humour, to be patient and tolerant whatever happens.

History tells us that the pioneers in the field have rarely been musicians and that the remedy was mostly empirical. But today, as with other therapies, it is obvious that music therapy should be applied only by expert hands in order to succeed and prove its worth.

This did happen in the United States as early as the First

7 THE MUSIC THERAPIST
A group of mentally handicapped children with Juliette Alvin

8 MUSIC BY PHYSICALLY HANDICAPPED CHILDREN—The Cup
Winners

9 THE VIOLA PLAYER

The player is a congenital left arm amputee. She wears an artificial arm with a skin rubber matching glove, rotary wrist and flexible fingers. The instrument is tuned in a reverse position thus enabling the right hand to play on the strings

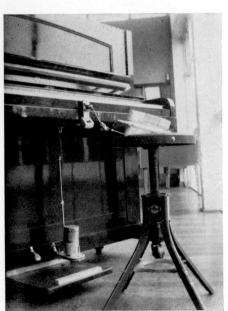

10 & 11 THE PIANIST

Gadget enabling a patient deprived of the use of her feet and legs to move the pedals through pressure from her back on a lever

World War, when professional musicians were hired by Veteran Hospitals as so-called 'music aides' and thus prepared the way for music therapy. Some good results attracted the interest of medical men and it was felt more and more that a specific training was necessary to make a therapist out of a musician.

In Great Britain, for a number of years, most of the work has been undertaken by various people whose musical knowledge and skill were sometimes too limited for them to use music as a therapeutic means under control, and this in spite of the unlimited devotion and enthusiasm which belong to the true pioneers. We owe them a debt of gratitude. So do we to the few musicians who first in the United States and more recently in Great Britain and elsewhere have blazed a trail and opened a way to the recognition of music therapy applied by specially trained people.

The term 'music therapy' has caught the popular imagination which, in an age of scientific vulgarisation, is impressed by anything with a medical connotation. The result is that a term which in itself should indicate a highly complex process has been misused and abused by a number of well-meaning people.

Working Conditions

In Great Britain as in the United States and elsewhere music therapy is used in a number of places concerned with ill people of all ages, namely hospitals for physical or mental disorder, rehabilitation centres, psychiatric social clubs, remedial and hospital schools, training day centres and so on. In each of these places the music therapist is playing a different part on his musical theme, each situation requiring a different technique. He may deal with maladjusted children or adults, delinquents, subnormal patients, cases of paralysis or spasticity, people of all ages with various kinds of education or background, each of them having a different attitude towards his illness and its treatment, each of them forming a personal relationship with the therapist, or being unable to communicate.

The work has to be conceived in order to fit not only the patient but the place in which the music sessions are held. In large hospitals with ambulatory patients music sessions may be organised in a special room or hall, or in the wards. They may also take place in small rooms in the case of small groups or for individual tuition. In orthopaedic hospitals the music therapist often has to work in the ward with bed-ridden or wheelchair cases requiring more individual attention.

When the patients are hospitalised one may expect a certain number of them to attend regularly the music-group sessions or their individual lessons, since the activities are usually held at a certain place at a certain time. But even so, many disruptions may occur and interfere with the therapist's work, for instance when a mental patient supposed to take a leading part is rendered totally ineffective by his drug treatment, or is too ill to come. Sometimes, unless the music sessions are specially earmarked, the patient may have to attend another more urgent therapy, or to perform a menial task, and is therefore absent.

This sort of situation is frequent in psychiatric social clubs, where attendance of the patients is voluntary and quite un-predictable. The therapist has to possess the ability to exploit fruitfully any unexpected situation and needs quick musical imagination to adapt himself and his techniques.

In Great Britain and some other countries the music therapist is still a pioneer and his acceptance depends on various human relationships. In any administration, from the high official to the lowest worker, the attitude of the staff influences all activities and at every level. The music therapist may find himself in a vulnerable position; he has to win the goodwill around, above and under him to be successful. He has to gain the co-operation of the nursing staff, the understanding of the medical staff and other therapists; he may even need the help of the domestic staff when his activities require certain practical amenities.

The same situation exists in a remedial school, a rehabilitation or training centre, when the music therapist has to make himself appreciated and win a place for himself among the medical and teaching staff, who may not be conversant with his therapeutic methods, or even have a conventional attitude towards music.

The Position in Great Britain

In spite of the difficulties every pioneer is bound to encounter, we find in Britain more than anywhere else a unique field for the use of music as a therapy with all kinds of people needing medical treatment, psychological help or social rehabilitation.

Britain has kept alive the Hellenic tradition that man's harmonious development cannot be achieved without the right balance between body and mind and that music is of special value in education. The tremendous development of amateur music in this country is not only culturally beneficial, it may be preventive of mental trouble.

The music therapist deals with sick people who as children have been accustomed to sing every day in the school assembly. Most adults remember some of the tunes to which they immediately respond, whenever or whoever they are. Some of them might have belonged to the school percussion band or orchestra. Unless it is undesirable to awake certain memories bound to past musical activities, the patient can be motivated to join in such activities, for which he may have retained a certain skill.

The new outlook on mental disorder has created new services for the day or ex-patient in various kinds of rehabilitiation centres. In such a setting the music therapist has to be socially oriented; his task is to help the patient to return gradually to community life. In Britain, from the village to the large city, all communities possess choirs and other amateur music-making groups functioning regularly. These can be of tremendous assistance in providing real stepping-stones in the process of social rehabilitation, from the informal sing-song in a psychiatric social club to a band or a fuller and more integrated music group. The music therapist may become a kind of social worker whose tool is music, and has to relate his work to the medical and social services available in the community.

Very few people are allergic or even totally indifferent to any kind of music. The man who has music in himself possesses against disorder and disharmony a means which can be therapeutic if he becomes mentally or physically affected.

Music therapy is teamwork, it should be connected with others such as physio-, speech- or psycho-therapy, or with occupational therapy, with which it should not be confused. We have indicated the different ways in which music can help these therapies; its contribution should be clearly stated in relation to the total treatment.

A number of modern specialists who have worked with a really skilled music therapist have come to the same conclusion as Dr Blair, that 'once a psychiatrist has become acquainted with the real potentialities of music therapy, he would deplore its absence from his therapeutic armament'.[1]

The two disciplines of medicine and music symbolised by Apollo are becoming increasingly receptive to each other. In recent years a number of physicians have addressed musicians on the value of music therapy. Music therapists have been invited to discuss the subject with the medical and nursing staff of various hospitals. A third discipline has now become involved, namely remedial education. Educationists, psychologists, pediatricians and musicians are trying to find a common philosophy in order to use the influence of music in the psychological and social

[1] Donald Blair, 'Music Therapy', *New Society*, 30 January 1964, p. 26.

maturation of the handicapped child. This work with the young requires not only generous and devoted hands but a working mind directing them on a basic knowledge of child development. The music therapist has to be conversant with learning processes and remedial methods in order to find the musical techniques adaptable to the child and his handicap.[1]

Conclusion

We may conclude that real music therapists in any country are necessarily rare, since they are not merely born but made out of much acquired knowledge and experience.

Ultimately the musicians entrusted with patients are responsible for the development of music therapy as a rational means in the fight against disease of mind and body, a fight which is no longer fought single-handed, but involves numerous and specialised techniques.

Music, born of the primeval element of sound, captured by man, and by him organised, has become his servant, his benefactor and sometimes his master.

The dynamic and emotional, the primitive and spiritual forces that music integrates can serve man today in the battle of the body and of the mind, as they have done since time immemorial.

[1] J. Alvin, *Music for the Handicapped Child.*

Index